Simple Annals
200 Years of an American Family

Simple Annals

200 *Years of an American Family*

By Robert H. Allen

≈

Let not Ambition mock their useful toil,
Their homely joys, and destiny obscure
Nor Grandure hear with a disdainful smile
The short and simple annals of the poor

Thomas Gray
"Elegy Written in a Country Churchyard"

≈

FOUR WALLS EIGHT WINDOWS
NEW YORK/LONDON

Published in the United States by:
Four Walls Eight Windows
39 West 14th Street, room 503
New York, N.Y., 10011

U.K. offices:
Four Walls Eight Windows/Turnaround
Coburg Road, Wood Green
London N22 6TZ England

First printing April 1997.

Library of Congress Cataloging-in-Publication Data:
Allen, Robert H. (Robert Howard), 1949-
Simple Annals: 200 Years of an American Family/by Robert H. Allen.
p. cm.
ISBN 1-56858-090-8 (alk. paper)
1. Folklore—Appalachian Region, Southern—Poetry. 2. Family—Tennessee—History—Poetry.
3. Allen, Robert H. (Robert Howard), 1949-   —Family—Poetry.
PS3551.L4156S56 1997
811'.54—DC21
          96-45312

     CIP

1   0   9   8   7   6   5   4   3   2   1

Printed in the United States

In memory of Donald Davie
Who taught me how to write poetry

Preface

This is a collection largely based on family legends and folk tales that I heard when I was a child in rural West Tennessee. Most of them are about my mother's side of the family. Generally, I have tried to retell the tales not as I heard them, but to convey something of what it was like to hear these tales. I have taken liberties with names and facts, as is every poet's right.

The stories are arranged in roughly chronological order, beginning with the Revolution and coming down to my own life, my time as a graduate student in Nashville, and my search for information on my father's side of the family. The book is thus autobiographical in its reliance on actual occurrences and people and the things they said and did.

In a larger sense, it is autobiographical in that it is a sort of road map to the basic geography of my mind. Much of my character, my slant on life, was formed by these stories, the values they convey.

Autobiographies in general suffer from the flaw of self-indulgence. I hope to have escaped that trap by writing mostly about other people. The work is also intended to some extent to be a memorial to the persons the poems are about, and a memoir of sorts on the customs, character and beliefs of the old West Tennesseeans. They are long dead, those pioneers, and have left few if any heirs who will be embarrassed at these words.

—Robert Allen
Martin, Tennessee
October 1996

I
BEGINNINGS

Elias Butler

(1750–1836)

I.

Jim was crying when I came home,
A turkey for supper bleeding down my back.

Jim, but not like a child. I knew
The old story had found me when I saw the smoke
In the grey woods where I thought
There was only God and the sun and the rain.

And my heart was in me
Like a live coal swallowed.

Grandfather was a lawyer on the coast,
At Chowan where the sea
Washes up the chaff of ships
And men, and laws.

In his temper he could burn the air
With oaths, and did, cursing Governor Eden
For a hand in Bluebeard's pocket.

My father, for perhaps no more reason
Than to be his own man, was mild,
Quiet as the sunset, loving
God and a few books.
                              But he signed
The petition against the Irregularities—

The corruptions that crept into our laws—
Putting his honor to it. His name
Went for all, as honest men's do.

"I'm writing," he said
"An honest man to my honest king."

Honest. But he'd have died for it
When his other signers
Took their guns
To back their pens.

                         I was twelve then.
We ran, father, mother, my brother, I
From the city on the bay—

The river
Holds a round of muddy water
Like a mirror,
Dirty, the image
Of London, Paris, Rome
Small within it—

But what of me?
Third in the line that I remember,
Jim there, forth, then his children, and theirs—
A new beginning? the howl
That cuts his throat. . .

I kept to his ways,
That quiet man,
                    wanting

No politics, protests, petitions; I thought
We'd left that all behind
Where the road faded out.

The place we stopped
Was trees and water
No name yet on it.

Birdsong, the wind,
Water laughing
Down the bare stone breasts
Of old mountains.
                    Mine.

We lived
By the blade of an ax that cleared for corn,
By the tongue of the plow that broke the earth,
By the crack of the gun that brought home meat.

I set
The laughing water turning
Millstones on wheat,
And it prattled like my children—farmers gathered—
Was this my sin—
A taking from the world?

They have caught up with me.
I am their heir.
                    What have they done?

What's in the house, boy,
That you have seen

And do not want me to see?

Dead. Elizabeth. Wife. Mother. Murdered.

Because she would not give them meal.

Redcoats with Hessian knives
On their flintlocks.
                    For women?
There was no meal.
Don't the fools know that?
Green took it to feed his Continentals.

I had to hunt to feed my family.

Don't they speak English,
Soldiers of the English king.

He saw it. The words
Are in his throat, no sobbing
Will get them out.

My mill burnt.
My millstones cracked in the heat.

                    I have to bury her,
Then fight against my king.

II.

So long ago, now, I remember,
Betty found wild roses
And put them on the box.

I moved when time
Seemed not to, like a puppet.
Something else, call it
The violence of the time,
Pulled the strings.

I went to General Lillington:
"I want to fight."
                        He
Looked me through, asked questions:

Forty years old.
Six children.
Wife dead.
Miller by trade,
Hands
Hard with tools.

                        I knew
I was no soldier, but I could not tell him why
I had to fight. Say it stuck
Like the words in my son's throat.

Then he looked in my eye. He must have seen
Men die when blood chokes them
Or their bowels are shot away.
But he could not stand my eye.

"I'll take you," he said,
General Lillington said,
And I thought I could kill or die.

But all it was, was work.
Carpenter, millwright,
They needed me for that.

Carving cogwheels, fitting hinges,
I fought by building a fort.
                        When the war
Ended and we were a nation
I had fired no gun, thrust no bayonet
Into an Englishman that might have killed my wife.

I was not sorry.
The black grief I held
                    clawing at me
Went into the forest.
As we had
When I was twelve.
And out of the woods
Where the water
Whispers and is strong
Came back life and love.

I married Sarah the year
Cornwallis surrendered.

I was born anew.
Six more children.

        My millwheel turned and the meal fell out.

III.
Where do the days go
That the sun grinds in the sky?

One day I was old
Before I had thought to be.

What rich flour
Is boltered from the chaff of our lives?

The sun turns in the sky
And pulls us westward

I went with my children to Tennessee.

The dry, dead, axle trees
Cry out as we climb
The raw bones of the Appalachians.
Stone. But living problematically,
Fleshed with trees,
Trickled down
With cold quick water.
                    I pity
The oxen toiling over the ridge of the world.

It's the labor of the world we're treading
Without rest on ten mountains or forty.

These mountains
Are like a fever and a chill.

The axles

Murmuring greenly
As the days turn over them.
The oxen
Snort steam, galled
In their castration.

Nights camped
Till the fire dies
And that lonely thing
Beyond the reach of every dying coal
Screams as though
It had a soul and that
Were chewed in the devil's mouth
Like a rotten tooth.

                    A miller still—
I eyed the granite
Bones of the hills
For the grey, speckled look
Of a good millstone.
                    And I never
Cupped my hands to drink
From the falling streams,
But I guessed at the power
Of this good water falling.

White with the dust of a bitter road
I yearned for the mill to be built again,
Yearned for corn where there is
A sea of trees and I to be
                    White with the dust of the bread
Of a settled life.

IV.

The wheel breaks; in my dream
It broke and I woke
Swimming in sweat, wanting Sarah
To comfort me like a child.

I was carving a bevel gear, that turns
The power flatwise spinning
Millstones upon the corn.

Beech wood like cheese
Curled off my blue steel chisel.

I came here, to Buena,
With my children who came
To clear new ground for corn,
In a place we came to name.
        In the wilderness
Jackson stole from the Choctaws.

They brought me like a keepsake
Wrapped in quilts,
        Like an old book
Full of mill plans and stories
To sit with great-grandsons.

Jim's boy, Bill
Dammed Maple Creek near the sleepy Sandy.
The gears grumble, the bolter paddles chaff.

"Being a miller's what made my hair white
Flour settles till it don't wash out."

Jimmy believed that,
Child that he was.

I talked politics and argued the Bible,
To neighbors, widened eyes
With stories of the Revolution;
Measured the toll, closed the shoot.

I was the axle
Nine children and thirty-eight grandchildren
Turned smoothly around.

                        In the dream
The chisel strays in the grain,
A crack opens, ruining the wheel.
I wake and in the woods
Something screams.

Reuben Burrow Wakes at Night

What I remember is the rhythm of the horse
In its walking, the clop, clop, clop
In gravel or mud or autumn leaves.

When you're old, you can't sleep—
Sleep is for young men beside their wives, and I
Am more than eighty,
An old man remembering.

Do you suppose
An infant in its mother's womb
Feels the rhythm of her walking,
Hears the beating of her warm heart
Up above for nine months like God?

It's that I feel—
The sway of a good horse under me,
Clop, clop, clop, while I rode
The circuits of God for forty years,
Prairie and woods,
Road and path,
Day and night,
Rain and sleet and snow,
Holding the Bible in the air
While my good horse swam the rivers.

Rain freezing my beard,
Or sun burning the back of my neck.

It's funny you know,
If you'd asked me, green and young,
What I thought I'd remember when I was old,
I'd've said the moment of salvation,
Or God's call to the pulpit or some fine thing.
But what I remember now, old, dying,
Yes, dying, is the sleepy sway
Of a good horse walking under me,
When I slept for hours in the woods at night,
Ol' Rahab following the road, faithful as a saint.

Ten thousand miles by careful guess
To preach God's word in half a dozen states
And four territories, to—maybe
A million souls. How many of them now
Are singing 'round God's seat,
Or will, for the riding
That has soaked into my bones.

Yes, dying,
In bed, in this dark room,
And unafraid.
I was never afraid,
Not in the great woods at night,
Not of Indians, bears,
Panthers. I knew
Behind each tree a legion of angels
With flaming swords drawn.
        And if I died,
An army of martyrs to meet me,
Christ leading them.

Should I fear now that all
Has been done—the "go preach"
Obeyed in a thousand backwoods towns?

No. The moon
Walks its slow old mare
Across the starry night.
                        And a rectangle of light
From my window creeps across the floor
In the shape of a grave.
                        I'm tired,
Rocked by my mother, I want to go
Lie down in the light.

Pioneer Bible

I write these words in the Bible
Where they will keep—
        my family
Among the families of God.

Jane married a Grey
They had three sons.

The Indians killed them at Paxton,
Except Newell, the youngest boy
Who lived though he was scalped.

> *Grooves cut in the bone*
> *On his naked skull*
> *So the flesh could grow back.*

I shudder, the ink
In the nub of the goose quill
Turns cold, flows like blood
On the white bone of the child of my child.

Joshua moved to New Madrid
And has six children there.

> *It's a place like this, he says*
> *Fields set in the woods,*
> *Walls against the wilderness,*
> *Fireplaces, cups set on raw wood tables.*

He does well. Anne married a man
Who wastes more than he makes,
Whoremongering, fighting, drinking—
Throwing away coins
Free as the spots on dice.

She has five children
And lives somehow
And loves him
And is better than any of us.

Draw a line under the column of figures,
Three and six are nine,
Touch the five five times counting—
Fourteen grandchildren.

The woods are being cleared.
Twelve will live after me,
And one will inherit this Bible,
Keep it maybe to know
Whose kin they are
Where they come from.

The Seventh Tennessee Cavalry, Federal

Horses, galloping—
We rode with Hawkins
For Lincoln, Union
And the hell of the thing.

We left the creeping plow
And the birds following
To graze the petty worms
For galloping, the wind
In our faces, to war.

We slept beside our horses
Or slept in the saddle
While the nights moved
Troops of stars across the sky.

Alabama, Kentucky, Georgia,
States we never thought to see,
We galloped over, hooves
Striking fire as we rode.

Horses, the rattle
Of their running, the smell
Of them, their neighings
Filled our waking and our dreams.

The world was wider
        Than any field we had cleared;
        We rode farther

Than any town we'd traded in.

Horses running
Down a string of towns,
To skirmishes, battle, Oh and
The silent dead of peace.

The Seventh Cavalry in Kentucky

John Singleton Speaks

Pa Haywood and his wife were both
Kind as family to us when we stopped
Outside of Benton, waiting for the road to dry.
We asked to camp out in their field, they said
To take their barn long as the rain fell cold;
We in turn left all our matches in their hands
And slept on hay, dry and warm between the cows.

But when we came back though we heard the rebs
Had billeted themselves on those old folks,
Had shot their livestock, eating what they could
And left the rest out in the fields to rot.
Ma Haywood ran to meet us, crying as she ran.
We found her husband sitting on his porch
Watching the buzzards, empty eyed, that milled
Like great black leaves in a whirlwind caught.
He said they would be back by dark
To take his bed and cuss his wife and let
Their captain use his coffee pot
To piss in through that night.
                                                We said
That they would not—that word
Put light back in his eyes.

We laid an ambush up the road beyond the reach
Of bullets, where the logs had fallen 'long the road.
Then waited while the sun sank down among
The winter-naked trees whose opening buds

Reminded us that we should be at home
Plowing fields.
                        And then they came,
Their horses' hooves in clay a-sucking mud,
Some of the grey-coats singing songs
We knew. And when they passed a rotten stump
We all sprang out, each picking one to shoot.
All hell was loose, and those five minutes hung
For hours like a great bird's wing between its beats.
The horses screamed and reared and fell and took
Their riders down with them. Men cussed,
Broken bones gleamed white out of wounds
Still pumping heart's blood.
                        And it was done.
They all rode off shooting wild. Some two
Upon a horse, some shot and trailing blood.

We all jumped out and cheered and called them dogs
And laughed; but sudden as the ambush had been sprung
We looked around and saw that one of us
Had not stood up to cuss and laugh:
Old Asa Hampton's youngest son who hid
Behind a log to shoot his reb.
I found him first and for as long as it might take
A bird to sing five notes I thought he was asleep
As I had seen him sleep a thousand mornings in the camp.
But there was blood a-pouring out of him
Through one small hole no bigger than a dime.
I thought if I but stopped it with my thumb
He would stand up and mock the rebels where they ran.
But no. He never spoke a word or groaned.

Then when the bleeding stopped a cold sweat covered
                              him
Although the air was frosty cold. Six of us ran
With Lonnie Hampton limp between our arms
Back to the Haywood farm; that night when two
Struck on their mantle clock, he died. Ma wept
For him as though he were her son.
We buried Lonnie Hampton with the Haywood dead
Behind their home. And when the sun stayed out
Five days to dry the road we rode away.

Rebeccah Singleton Thomas
(1826–1891)

John Barber came in muddy boots to bring
A pheasant hen a-dripping blood for Pa
Because he had been sick in bed for many days.
Now Ma had gone to Boydtown for medicine
So I, thinking I was nigh grown, cooked it
For Pa and let it burn, because Pa called
And wanted me to come and help him turn.
But when he saw his supper burnt he drew
The last breath that he ever was to breathe
And let it out a-cursing me to God and Christ.

Then Ma was sitting by the fire
One night when all we children slept,
Stirring the ashes with her stick.
She looked and there was Pa in there
His beard all bristling out on him,
His face made out of flame, all hell
In his eyes, looking back at her.

We left that house, that farm, that state behind
Where my three brothers all had grown up wild
And trudged the mountains whose shoulders brush
The clear blue sky, to come to Tennessee.
I met my Richard here, a troubled, sad
Religious man, and married him. We had
Nine children born before the war and all
But one had lived

He hated slavery, but then who
Would feed that many mouths
If he took off to fight the rebs?
And then there came one awful day
When rebel press gangs were coming by;
He sat at the wood pile with the ax
Swearing that he would cut off
His left hand if they came to take him.

There was nothing could be done but hide,
So Richard and some other men from there
Who thought they had more part with their own kin
Than they had with Lincoln and the War dug out
A hiding place into a hill-side in the woods,
Stocked corn and meat out there and quilts
And ran there if they heard of soldiers near.

Then one day John Brinkley came
With his band of drunks and rascals
That called themselves Confederates,
With not so much as a grey coat
To bless their mangy backs and asked
Where Richard was—he was worth
Five dollars to those bitches' sons.
And when I wouldn't tell them where
He was they took my youngest boy
David, not six years old by then
And stood him on the eating table
A noose around his little neck.
"I guess you'll tell us now," he said.

But I was mad as hell. "I've got
Three brothers wearing blue, and they all know
     Your names and where your families live," I told
     That dog. "Now leave my house and kids in peace
Or when the Singletons come back from war
There will not be a Brinkley left alive
To rue the day that you dared to touch my son."

And I drilled holes in him with my eyes
That can back down a snarling dog.
And Johnny Brinkley and his fools
Rode off and never said a word.

Josiah Bateman

Old Josiah Bateman's buried over there—government marker—he was in the War. I've heard him talk about it a many a time, him and Mark Hallmark and old John Singleton used to set out in front of the store there at Dollar and talk about the War. I'd set and listen to 'em all day. They was with Hawkins when he surrendered. Warn't no use of it neither, they could have beat that rebel. I've heard John Singleton say he set down an' cried when he found out that Hawkins had surrendered them. They sent 'em to Andersonville. Put 'em down in a pit and treated 'em worse than they would have treated animals. I've heard John Bateman say he seen a man gnaw the flesh off of his shoulder he was so hungry. They'd throw a dog down in there and the men'd fight over it, tear it up and eat it alive. Well, old Josh warn't never much for going to church, but I remember one time he did go. Eb Hampton and his girls, they was all by his second wife, was singers and one day they was singing at Mount Comfort during the revival. It was a hot summer day and there was flies ever'where. So Old Josh, he gets on the front bench there, right in front of the singers and he commences to make out like he was catching flies and popping 'em in his mouth. 'Course they had to stop singing and start laughing. That was old man Bateman alright, eh!

In Old Nineveh

I was in the store at Nineveh
When Boney Hampton was there selling
His Patent Mole Traps and Darnals come in.

   They say that Boney Hampton had them take
   Bill Darnals out in his yard
   And hang him there right in front
   Of his wife and little son,
   Because he thought he was a spy.

The War was ended twenty years
            But Nathan Darnals did not think that it
            Had any end while the rebel lived
            Who killed his father in cold blood.

So in he came walking his shotgun down his leg
And stood over old man Hampton for a minute
Looking him in the eye. Then shot him dead.

Walked out the store, straddled the fence
Around a field, leaning his gun
And walked away across the field
Leaving his shotgun there.

II

IN A QUIET PLACE

The Lonesome Remember

The lonesome remember—memory
Is their consolation—for others
Life: the flesh, battle, all, and then
Someone lonesome will walk
Through a graveyard and point
                  At a stone and remember
                Stories of lust, anger, sorrow
             That hurt no more. There are two
Worlds: one bright and terrible
As the fall of true words, one
Futile as the hiding of dead flesh
Under clay when above the dust of dust
There strolls in twilight some poet
Who carries it all and walks
Free, light, owning the heroes
Who dance and die as the words
Will, to some song, maybe
Whispered over old marble by the wind

A Sense of Place

A tornado picked up his house, scattered it like straw,
Landed him unhurt in a ditch.
He shook his fist at the leaving storm, and,
"Aye God, you can blow me away,
But you'll strike a knot when you hit Round Top"
(Meaning a certain prominent hill).

The mother of four blind children
Taught them to hoe their rows
By putting their toes around the bean plants
And cutting down everything else;
But one day when they left
A neat and perfect row of weeds
She covered her face with her apron, wept,
Went back and replanted her beans.

Pneumonia took her husband before the Civil War
        could;
Guerrilla raiders took her only two horses,
        a mare and a colt.
There was nothing left, nothing
But her twelve year old daughter to pull the plow,
                Her six year old son to guide it.

But they lived, generation by generation on the
        hard land,
Under the hot sun, the still,
Unanswering stars; and I
Was born among them,

,

Therefore ought
To laugh at all
Storms, weep
At the bottomless pathos of life,
And pull the plow in my manner
With poor words, orphaned and heir
And son of such.

The Cradle

Walnut carved smells,
Drawblade whisks clean. Brace on breastbone
Auger drilling for pegs.
                              Pa
Cutting a cradle for his firstborn.
Sawblade eating straight down the grey pencil mark
The first daughter never married and handed him
The last drink of water he ever drank
Boards tongued and grooved
To fit tight as the grain
The first son came nearly blind,
Worked hard and died young
Rasp rounding rocker
Smooth as the flanks of a racing mare
A genius at math and music, a storekeeper, Opp
Squared and carved, mortised and tenoned
Ida. She sat by the fire, blind
Stirred the ashes, listened to stories
Peg trimmed, tapped home
Head split and wedged
Lindie, twice married
She buried a husband and an only child
Pattern of lathe-bite on the ends of posts
Medie, blind, beautiful
Dead at twenty
                    Plain lisping shaving
                    Lillie died in Pa's arms
Walnut ribbons piling on the floor
Lorie felt for his toys

And died in the cradle
Pattern the chisel cuts
Jim read almanacs
The Bible
Dance of cut leaf on hard wood
Ed in anger
Cut off his toe at eight,
Lay for months with his foot hanging out
Of the cradle that Pa was making
Pattern in grey lead on hard black wood
Shape of a cradle for a family unborn.

John Slickum

He'd Pa's big nose,
> the bald head of his father's people
> the frame of the Thomas men,
> big bones dangling loose in a sack of skin
> half-blind eyes and a long face under them
> that was sad as the worn-out fields.

He'd a bad wife:
> who was always imagining
> that she was sick with something,
> was always wanting some fancy thing,
> and was always having him leave
> his shoes outdoors when the weather was cold.

He'd a bad life:
> He carried his son on his shoulders
> When the boy was eight, so he could
> tell John Slickum where to put the ax
> when he cleared Tate's Bottom of the brush.
> John died of cancer at fifty, silent in the pain.

Uncle John,
If God kept you
From the snakes when you cleared the creek banks,
What can He do for you now?

Siney and the Stockings

Women used to kirtle up their knitting in their aprons when they went visiting. Then they'd set there and knit while they was talking. Visit the whole day and there they have their knitting done. Well, one time old Siney Smothers come over—that was Uncle Will's mother and Aunt Marth's—she was a McGhee from Old Nineveh. Her and Ma was asitting there with the fireplace behind 'em. Well, Ma had took off her stockings and hung 'em up on the spinning wheel there by the fire. Well, Sis was always full of her devil, so she slipped around and just as easy as she could she started turning the spinning wheel. And them socks moved over on the band till they was right behind ol' Siney's head. She was so curious she couldn't live—a mighty particular old woman. Well, she smelled them hot stockings hanging right behind her and she commenced to pull up her nose and let on she smelled something. Finally she come out and said, "Tabby," she said, "there's a dead hen under the house."

Opp

Only sound was the wagon
Groaning like a troubled sleeper
Down red-clay roads
Between cut fields
Through autumn-naked woods

And the blind old mare
Nickering now and then
Her feet a steady pounding
Slow and unforgiving as the winter rain.

And then he busted out crying
And there were more tears in him
Than you'd think a ten-year-old could hold.

And it was all that he didn't want to go.

He didn't want to go
Bright as he was
                    To blind school in Nashville.

Ma held him in her lap,
His wet and blind and miserable face
Hid from the sky and God
By her blue apron.

And her hand upon him could not stop
His dry heaving. And she could not stand
The lonely grief of her son.

"Turn the wagon 'round."

They missed the train at Buena.

Opp became a storekeeper.

It was left to me to tell the story.

Opp Speaks

Isaac Hallmark's tobacco barn burned down
From the fire that was a-curing the leaf
And Pa found me nails among the ashes
And I played at building things as best I could
Being nearly blind. From a cigar box
I made a fiddle and the music woke
At my finger tips. A wild dancing
And drinking was in my Baptist blood.
Sister Lindie read me
Books of mathematics and algebra
And in my dark, blurred world
Bright forms took shape, clear-edged
As a straight-razor; prime numbers
Thinning out as they rise like leaves
On the trees I could not see; digits
In pi stretching far ahead like the roads
            I could never run; squares and roots
            Piling up like chords in "Soldier's Joy"
Or "Bonaparte's Retreat." I played for dances
Not telling Ma who always said
"You can dance into hell, but you can't
Dance out again."
            I kept a store
For forty-three years, and it kept me—
Selling chickens that Jim and Edd
Bought, door-to-door in an A-model truck,
Crossing their wings on their backs
To weigh them on a handheld scale;
Selling eggs that Lindie and Sis

Penciled their names and addresses on,
Mentioning that they were single.
I cast up the accounts in my head
And I forgot much when neighbors I knew
Could not pay, for to dance parties and liquor
And to Nan I owed much.

Con Green

It was for Nan I always thought
And because Con Green was a bastard born
And lived alone with his old mother there
In the old house that Monroe Cary built.

He went with Nan, washed and dressed and combed
The way he never was. But Opp who kept
A store married her and fed that gang of kids
Her first husband had left her with alone.

Con Green when sober was as good a man
As most men are; he worked hard with me
When we were clearing ground for Amos Clay,
But whiskey's what he bought the day we all got paid.

His mother could have kept him quiet but she
Was off in Benton County at her sister's house.
So Con got crying drunk and lay out on his porch
And yelled at every passer by that Opp
Had got Nan pregnant just so she'd marry him.

The sun went down on him as he lay there
And fell asleep, and cold dew fell on him;
But when he woke his drunk temper was hot;
He fumbled in his empty house and found his gun.

Con stumbled down the gravel road
To Opp's store in the dark and stood out front
And cursed the still night air hot blue

With every vulgar word he knew,
Rotten teeth and sour-mash both on his breath.

Then he commenced to shoot into the store
Too drunk to aim, though empty windows and locked door;
He shot up the benches on the porch and shot
The thermometer off the post.

And fell down crying; and the sheriff found him wet
With tears and dew and his own piss
And took him to the jail for the night
And put him safe to bed.

Lige Autry and the Comb

Lige Autry was a big preacher. I don't reckon there was a bigger one in the world. He died in the pulpit there at Mount Comfort—come in to preach one morning, said he didn't feel too well, and before he's done he just fell dead there in the pulpit—they kept his picture hanging on the wall for I don' know how long, there behind the amen corner. Well, anyhow, one time Lige Autry went to one of his church member's house. They had a big family Bible there that they kept in the front room, and all the time they was talking, they was telling Lige how much they read the Bible, read it ever' day. Well, when the woman of the house called supper, he stayed behind, making like he was reading that big Bible. He took out his comb and put it in the Bible, closed it on it there. Then after supper he made like he'd lost his comb, had 'em hunting ever' where. 'Course they couldn't find it. Well, then a year later, he was visiting the same family, and they was bragging again about how much they read the Bible, how they didn't let a day pass without reading some in it. "Oh," Brother Autry said, "did you ever find that comb I lost back when I's here last time?" "Why, no, never did, Brother Autry." So he opened the Bible, and there it was.

Aunt Ida

Keys without locks and locks without keys.
                    —Eugène de Saint Exupéry
                              The Wind, the Sand and the Stars

Keys.
     I remember keys.
In hands withered and softer than membrane.
Counting, on the mnemonic of keys,
Stories. . . . .
        Aunt Ida.

Her last courtship
Was when she was seventy.
Mr. Parkes came over
And she glittered
               in her second-hand sequin dress.

The doctor who treated her hernia, later,
Remarked that she was a virgin.

My mother, almost,
I lived my childhood
And hers too, nearly,
     history of the family
     gossip of a neighborhood
Gone now
A hundred years.

Her trunk
     that stank of old cloth. In the tray

Cancer of green on brass brooches.
Needles rust clotted.
Beeswax aged black.
Photos, buttons and T-model spark-plugs.

Her bitterness,
                    how she resented
Every slight
The grudges she carried
Till she was hunchbacked.

In this
My mother,
Too, almost.

All things kept,
Good, bad
The endless world
Twined in a ball of words.

    She sat by the bed
When I was afraid of the dark,
            And remembered on the click of the keys
            That she took from her flowery apron pocket:

"This was Pa's house key;
                    When I was little. . . ."
                    "This went to Medie's trunk.
 One time she set down on a wasp. . . ."

    then left me in the dream
To lock the doors

Checked windows
The house safe.

                Between waking and dreaming, still,
I think I hear her shuffling away
To tend the doors
With the keys.

Aunt Ida's Hair

It's getting grey now and that's the third color it's been. They say, though, you'll never be whiteheaded if you's ever redheaded and I was redheaded as a pecker-wood when I was a girl. One time Aunt Calline Bateman come to stay with us. She was Granma Thomas' sister—married Henry Bateman—he died right after the War and Aunt Calline stayed around with her folks after that. She's a big, fat woman, like Granma and nasty! She never would change her dress—she wore one dress over the other and when one of 'em got too dirty she'd just pull it off and there was another dress under that. She dipped snuff and there was always a ring of snuff around her mouth—never did wash nor nothing.

Well, she slept on my bed. I had a little old trundle bed—rolled back under Pa and Ma's big bed during the day. That was that big old bed of theirs Pa made when they first got married, called it the Horny Bed. Aunt Calline stayed with us sev'l weeks and I slept on a pallet on the floor.

Well, after that Aunt Calline went to stay with Uncle Zer—heh! she didn't stay long though, cause Aunt Mary couldn't put up with her—poor old thing!—Aunt Mary was awfully curious—she had her ways. So I went back to sleeping on my little trundle bed, and first thing I knowed I had head lice. Aunt Calline had left 'em in the bed you see. Well I done ever' thing I knowed to get rid of them head lice—washed my head with lye soap and ever' thing. Finally somebody told me to wash my head with coal oil and that would kill 'em off. Well, I took a quart of coal oil and I went down to the spring and I done it. And shore enough ever' hair on my head fell out. I'se as bald headed as a watermelon there, but it was in the summer time. Come to grow back, it growed in black—just as black as a crow and I'd had the prettiest red hair 'fore that—took after Pa's folks, they was all redheaded. An' that's how come me to be getting the third color of hair now. They say, though, that you'll never be whiteheaded if you'se ever redheaded, and that's why it's coming in in streaks. Killed them lice, though.

The Three Little Pigs

(exactly as Ida told it)

One time there was a old sow and she had three
       little pigs.
And that old sow said to them three little pigs:
"What'd you'll do if I'se to go off and die?"

The fist little pig he says:
"I'd build me a house outta sand."

The second little pig he says:
"I'd build me a house outta bark and sticks."

The third little pig says:
"I'd build me a house outta bricks."

Well, that old sow went off and died.
And the little pigs built their houses like they said
       they would.

Then along come the old fox.

The old fox he commence to rooting around
       the sand house
And he rooted it down and eat that little pig.

Then the old fox he commence to rooting around
       the house of sticks and bark
And he rooted it down and eat that little pig.

Then the old fox he commence to rooting around the
     house of bricks,
But he just hurt his nose.

So the old fox he thought to hisself,
"I'll just wait around till that little pigs comes out
     to go to the spring."

Well, sure enough, long about dusky dark
That little pig come out to get him a bucket of water,
And the old fox grabbed him.

The little pig said:
"If you'll let me go down to the spring and get a bucket of
water,
I'll make us some mush."

Well, the old fox thought:
"I'll have me some mush
And then I'll have me a pig to eat."
So he let him go get his water.
Well, the little pig come back to the house
And put the water on to bol.

          Then along about time it commence to boiling
               The little pig says, "Do you hear that?"

               "Hear what?" the old fox says.

"Hear them foxhounds a-barking and them hunters with
them," the little pig says.

"Foxhounds!" the old fox says,
"They'll get after me!
Hide me, hide me quick."

"Jump in this here trunk,"
The little pig said.

The old fox, he jumped in that trunk.

The little pig, he slammed the lid down on the trunk
And locked it. Then he got that boiling water
And commence to pour it down through the cracks in
     the trunk.

"Ow, ow! there's fleas here," the old fox yelled,
"There's fleas here!"

What He Said

"She never loved me." The old voice came from far away,
From places dark and terrible as the grave. I saw more
Than I wanted to see.
                              A frail child
In a coarse cotton dress, sewn
From flour sacks and he was playing with her,
Stroking her limp blond hair.

She died. His first daughter
He could not
                    Let her go.
                    When his wife
              Turned needing flesh to fill the place
              She had birthed to the grave
He could not,
                              Seeing a little girl
                    Lying cold in the darkness.

She needed, to staunch
The grief that wasted out of her,
She needed.

She found another man.
Left with him.

He drank, throwing himself away, until he was senseless,
Walked the floor wailing, terrifying
His one son.
                    Then one day

She came back, ashamed—willing
To be what she could till she died,
Saying that she loved him.

She loved him.

The Buzzards

Me and Ellen Thomas used to play around all the time when we was girls. I remember one time Ma had made me the prettiest little dress. It was red checked stuff— Aunt Anne wove it herself. Had a little bow to go in my hair and ever' thing. We was staying with Uncle John, and me and Ellen was out playing. Ma told me not to get that new dress in anything. Well, from that Ellen figured she'd get me in something or she'd die. There was a nest of buzzards over there towards the Hale Rocks, so Ellen says, "Lets go over," she says, "and see them little buzzards." I didn't know no better, so I went with her, and I'se just a-holding my pretty new dress up ever' where, so it would get in the sawbriars nor nothing. We come to the big old tree where them buzzards had their nest and Ellen says to me, says, "Let's us climb up and look at them little buzzards." Well, we clomb the tree and there was them little buzzards plumb blind and naked. And just about the time we got there the old mother buzzard she come home. So she seen me there looking in her nest, and she flew down right over me and puked all over me. She'd been eating some dead cattle or something, I don't know what, and I got it all over me and all over that pritty checkered dress of mine. Went home, I reckon they smelled me coming half a mile.

Luther Lynch

When a calf broke his fence John Lynch
Gouged its eyes out
                    with his fingers
And when his horse
Could plow no more
He nailed it up in the barn
Let it starve.

Luther was his son
By his first wife, who, they said,
Was lucky when she died.

   Spring frogs, when they call
   Will look through ice again.
   The late frost drips off the twigs.
   The buds fall. No peaches
   No apples this year.

Luther's first job
Was toting water for the Dollar Steam Mill.

The buckets sloshed
And the water
Froze down his pant leg in winter.

   It gets so cold the trees split
   And your breath burns in you
   And the snow is white and the sky is white
   And nothing holds them part
   But a black line of trees.

He was coughing with TB
When he met Lindie
And loved her.
               They were married.

             When Daisy died at a year and a half
             Luther never cried. Asked Lindie not to cry:

"You'll have more to cry about
                   and soon."
                   It was ten days.

Luther coughed, growled
Drowned in his own blood.

    The corn's laid by.
    The sun in the field
    Is bright and hot as a plow colter.
    Locusts call at evening,
    "Pharaoh, Pharaoh."
    Revival time. We walk to church
    Carrying our shoes
    We walk to God.

She never remarried after that;
The last picture that we have of her
Is on the porch with her nieces and nephew.
The older one on the left
Is mother.

The Preacher's Britches

One time Taylor Boyd bought hisself a new pair of britches in Dollar, and come to get 'em home, they was too long. Well, that was on a Saturday and he was gonna preach the next day. So he asked his wife to cut 'em off for him. Well she was quilting on a quilt and she said she'd get to it. Come along in the evening and Miranda, she was still quilting and hadn't done nothing, so Taylor, he asked his daughter to cut his britches off for him. Well she was busy with something, but she said she'd get to it. Well, come along to bedtime and there was his britches and nobody had done nothing to them. So Taylor Boyd went to bed figuring he'd wear some old pair of britches to church the next day. Well, Miranda, she woke up in the night and it come to her mind that she'd promised to cut his britches off for him, so she got up and cut 'em off, hemmed 'em up good and all. Then later in the night, his daughter woke up and remembered she promised to cut off her daddy's britches for him. So she got up not a-knowing that her mother'd done done it, and cut his britches off too. Well, Taylor Boyd woke up Sunday morning and there was his new britches, cut off halfway to the knee! Plum ruint 'em, too.

Hands

He had let me hold a bar
Of P&G soap that was too big
For my bulky small hand
And play on the rub-board
Like I was washing clothes.

He had taught me language
With games and jokes—
   James E. Jones
   Grandfather.

        He held his hands
     A certain way when he was thinking

The thoughts
touched words
only here and there.

   I remember
How we changed places
In the dance of life, and he was my child.
And I worried that he wear
Clean clothes and not wander away
   Slept
With the doors locked from the inside

   How he would laugh
   Soft but cold
   As dead hands

And confide
His wild dreams
That were becoming real.

How could I not
Clean him when he fouled the bed
And hold his hands
And talk, not knowing
That he even heard?

Zade

Gone like the picture on a keepsake plate
That slips from soapy hands
And shatters on the floor—that
Was her family. Her father
Found other women, her mother
Scattered the hungry mouths
To her brothers who could feed them.

October there, I see her
In the twilight of some year,
Fading, that was gone
Before I was born, Zade, grandmother.

Open the past, peer in;
It is lit by light no eye living has seen.

In the back of a closet hangs a dress.
      See the dress in the October light
      Of a gone world, her dress,
   Grandfather could not let go when she died
   But kept it there in the embalmed light.

The light of the past is words, stories;
As she grew, twelve, fourteen, becoming a woman,
And leg-bones ached, not fitting her flesh
Her mother bought her a new spring dress
To cover her ankles, flowered poplin
Like the fields of blue cornflower and the wind.

She pinned the pattern cut from a newspaper
To the cloth and spread it on the bed, Zade did,
That girl who was to be my grandmother,
Cut round it carefully, left-handed
Just to fit—but when she lifted it up
There was with it a perfect shadow
Cut from her mother's chenille bedspread.

Shadows of a dress
In a gone light, an October light
Of all the past, shadow
Of a woman, thrown
As the low sun casts out long shadows
Across fields of fall flowers,
Grandmother whom I scarcely remember.

HER MOTHER'S SECOND HUSBAND

Now Albert Butler was a joker
And he liked to have his fun
Turpentining dogs in the streets of Buena
'Cause he liked to see 'em run.

One night the family was a-sleeping
Not a-thinking of any harm
'Cause the evening thunder'd blown 'round
And they wouldn't get no storm.

Albert Butler bust into the bedroom

Yelling, "Evy, jump and run!
There's a twister like a freight train a-coming
And it ain't gonna spare no one!

"Red lightning, hail, and winds a-screaming
With thunder to scare you deaf!
Run quick with the kids to the smokehouse cellar
Or we'll surely come to grief!"

So Ev she jumped up in a tremble
Wrapped little Zade in a sheet
Struck a light to the lamp beside her
And ran down in her bare feet.

And there was the sky all up above them
Fair to the stars on high
And Albert in the door behind her
A-laughing fit to die.

ఇ

He courted her in a buggy, grandfather
When he was a young man, the old man
Who was like a father to me. He was
Like so many young men I have known
Unsure of something, half-afraid,
            Running to women from it.

     He courted her in a buggy, the wheels
Frail as spiderwebs, it clattered over moonlit roads,
     Taking Jim and Zade to their future,

The wheels thin and delicate
As the wheel of stars that turn
Night by night soundless over the world.

The turning of the stars,
Water on the mill-wheel of time,
Laughter of the water of time as it falls,
Tears that humans mark their lives with,
They married on a day of rain.

Two children dead,
A trunk full of clothes
He would not open, and then
Her dress, empty, blackening with dust
In the back of a closet.

And he is gone, and I
Am the child that heard the stories,
A middle-aged man alone in a house
Like a boat capsized in the rain,
Remembering stories from an October light.

Fable

One time there was a old woman went to mill. Well, as she was coming home with her budget of meal tied up in a sack, it come up a big storm, it was lightning and thundering. Well, she went and got in the old church house there, stood in the door a-waiting for the storm to get over. One time it lightninged and she could see the devil up in the rafters at the back of the church house. Well, it was raining hard by then and she was afraid of the storm, so she says to herself, "I'll wait till the next time it lightnings, and then I'll leave." Well, next time it lightninged, she could see the devil again and he had moved up closer to her, there on the next rafter. Well, she says to her self, "I'll just wait for one more lightning flash to get over, then I'll leave." Then it lightninged again. And the devil got her.

Aunt Medie

Pa told Medie Lige Autry
Was coming to supper, a fine preacher,
And that he had a big nose,
and not to say
Anything about it.
Meaning no harm
She handed him the sugar-bowl with
"Would you choose some sugar
In you nose
Brother Autry?"
She was the prettiest of the Joneses
The line of her face
Clean and smooth
As the curves the martins cut
Flying in the sky at dusk.

A brain tumor killed her at twenty-one.
There was nothing the doctor could do
But give her morphine.

Pa used to quit plowing early
And go home by the graveyard
And stop and stare down at her grave.

A Horseman on the Bridge

(Jim speaks)

I was fourteen and thought myself
Much a man back then. That was when
Medie, my sister, was dying
Of a tumor in her brain.

Doc Massey only shook his head
And prescribed laudanum for her pain.
So we watched her sleep her life away
Or wake in agony and cry
Only to sleep again.

And then one night at dusky dark
Ma went for the bottle and found
That it had spilled and there was just enough
To let her sleep till midnight or so.
So one of us must go
To Buena and Doc Massey's house.

Well, Pa was sick with sitting up
And grieving for his girl
And I was the oldest boy
So I saddled Old Jenny and I rode.

I rode between the fields while night came on
And whippoorwills called from the woods.

A piece of yellow moon lit my way
When I came to the bridge at Garrettsburg.
But when I turned onto the bridge I saw

That there was a horseman standing there
Right in the middle of the bridge,
His head down, on his horse, a big black hat
                    Hiding all his face.

And he didn't move.
There was nothing for it
                    But I must ride by him on the bridge.

Jenny was shying and didn't want to go,
But I spurred her onto the bridge
And the clatter of her hooves
Was loud as thunder on the boards:
                    I thought that it would wake the dead,
                    But the man on the horse never moved.

I rode right past him there
But could not make myself
Turn and look at him
Or speak.
        And it was cold
Right over the water, like I rode
Through some piece of winter there.

                    Then when I'd passed him by
I put the spurs to Jenny good
And rode like hell was behind me
                    Till the bridge and the river were out of sight.

I woke Doc Massey, got the laudanum
And rode back home the long way 'round.

Next night, past midnight, Medie died.

Jim a-Courting

I went over to Ben Gooch's for Sunday dinner one time—that was when I'se courting Mandy and come to set down to eat, her old mammy tuck the biscuits and put 'em in a basket, kept 'em in her lap—anybody wanted a biscuit she'd reach down there and pass 'em one. I didn't know what to think of them.

Well, I'd 'bout decided to marry Mandy and I bought her a set a' vases and bowl of the prettiest Carnival glass—give nearly fifty cents for 'em at Opp's store. I'se gonna ride over and propose to her that Sunday. Well, come Friday I got a letter from Mandy—said her Daddy had promised to buy her a parlor organ if she wouldn't have nothing to do with me. She always wanted a parlor organ and she'd tuck him up on it. Give them vases to Zade when I married her. They was curious people, them Gooches was, cur—riss, I tell you.

Pa Buys Salt

One time me and Will drove over to Perryville to buy salt—that was right after the War and salt 'us scarce—people used to dig up the dirt under their smokehouses, boil it in a washpot, then pour off the water, and boil that down to get back the salt that had been spilled.

We bored a hole up in the underside of the wagon tongue, put our money up in there and put a stopper in it, so if there was any bushwhackers stopped us, they couldn't find our money. We crossed Tennessee River there at the Puryear Ferry, and got our salt. There was hoop snakes over there in Perry County—we'se coming downhill one time and one of them took out after us—put its tail in its mouth and rolled down that hill like the rim of a wagon wheel—went right past us, on down the hill. I seed a joint snake too—put together in joints, like cane. I hit at it with a stick and it scattered in a hunnert pieces. Later on, they'd come back together.

Well, when we come back to the river it come up a cloud and me and Will run and got in a hollow oak tree there by the river. Biggest tree I ever did see. So big in there I took a sixteen-foot fence-rail and held it out level and I could turn plum around in there. And if you don't believe it, you can ask your Uncle Will.

Cousin Steed

"I'm eighty-six years old
                And I seen ever' thing:

    I've seen some things meant ever' thing to me
And I seen some things I'd a give the world not to see.

God put me here for something,
I don't know what, but that's how come I'm alive today."

Hampton

I jes' barely remember Ol' Ebb Hampton. He was a old, old man when I was a little girl. Him and his daughter Rosey and his daughter Lindie used to go around, sing at churches. They was awful religious folks. Old Ebb died with a cancer on his face. They had put him up in a screen-wire cage to keep the flies from a-blowing him, 'fore he died.

Lim and Abe was his boys—they was both of them so 'fraid of women, woman was to come to their house, they'd fight each other to see who could get up the chimbley first. Well, after Lim married, Abe bought him a house there in Buena Vista; place was hainted. One day he was out in the stable and he heard the ghost a-mumbling something—mumbling and mumbling. Well, Abe said to it, "In the name of Jesus, speak to me," and he said that three times and the ghost had to answer him— told him to go over there in the south corner of the stable and dig there—and sure 'nough there was a iron dinner kettle full of gold money.

Mart Butler

I loved him and I swear to God I wouldn't a-done it,
Slapped him when he was sucking at my breast
And bit my nipple with his little teeth, and drew
The blood—not for my soul would I a-done it.

And after that he was dumb and foolish and drooled
Warm spit and had to be watched or he would fall
Into the fire or roll off the bed if he was left alone,
So we put him a cage in the front room, where he slept.

It seems like I could reach out, if I only could
Reach far enough, and grab that moment when I hit
My little son—but like a wild bird that flies
Into the house and beats itself to death on the wall
I cannot quite catch that time—still my arm goes back
And still my milk-swelled breast hurts sudden
As Mart's soft head jerks away, and all the world
Bears in on him and reason's just lit wick
Smothers in the wind out forever.

Jim Thomas

Martha's in the barn loft
Rolling like a stormy sea
Under a man,

And Tirece, my daughter,
Her daughter, is somewhere by my bed
Crying to break her heart,

       While I lie here, Jim Thomas,
In my thirty-first year,
Dying of typhoid fever.

I knew it all, knew it sure
As if I were God and looked
       Down from cool heaven

And saw my wife for another man
Leaving my sickbed side,
Leaving the spoon in the soup bowl

To foul the hay in the barn loft
With worse than the horses
Left to themselves might do.

That's why I ate
The greasy meat my daughter
Cooked at my bidding—

Fine fried sausage

That burst my fevered guts
And let my life out.

So now I'm dying and feel
So far from all that
Sorryness and sorrow

That I think my life
No more than one of the tales
Mama told us children

At the end of a day's hard work when the fire
Was dying out, and the shadows
Gathering like snow near our beds.

Aunt Marth

Aunt Marth warn't no 'count. Reason Uncle Jim died was a'cause of her. She was fooling round with Wash Allen and she left him at home by hisself with the children when he had typhoid fever. He told Tirece, that was his oldest girl, that he wanted some sausage. Well, she was just a child and she didn't know no better, so she went and fried him some. He eat 'em and that killed him. You can't eat nothing like that when you got typhoid—your guts get thin as silk paper. They say when he died Aunt Marth was up in the barn loft with Wash Allen.

They scattered the kids after that. Uncle Zer took one, Aunt Anne and Uncle Will took one, Uncle John raised Tirece—she had a crooked neck, bent round to the side. Aunt Marth lived around any way she could. When she died they brought her over to Uncle John's, but Aunt Ad wouldn't let her in the house. They had her in her coffin, gonna set up with her. So they put her out on the front porch that night and buried her the next day. Ma said if they'd a brought her to her house she'd 'a let 'em brought her in and set up with her like they should. Said it didn't matter—she's dead. They buried her by Uncle Jim, there in the family row and Tirece is the next one over.

Ed Loses a Race

I told Gabe Hallmark I'd win the race
But then forgot all that
And stopped out in the woods and stared at her.

I knew her when she married
Dan Williams. Then the children
Came quickly, a boy, two girls.

I took the side road,
A faster way, but hilly
And there around a curve,
Wearing blue in the moonlight
She stood with her back
                To that great oak.

My horse stopped before I could rein him to.
And I stood and looked at her
While Gabe won the race and waited for me.

She smiled as natural as she'd smiled before
She died in childbirth with her fourth.

When I told Dan the next day,
He shook his head in no surprise
And told me all his kids
Said their mother often came to them
In the woods and played with them,
                Sang them songs and plaited
                Wildflowers for their hair.

I stood up in my saddle in the woods
And nothing moved, not a cricket
                              Called, not a leaf
                    Fell down from any tree,
                    Staring at a face I'd last seen
                    Closed in a coffin three years before.

She had a little budget at her feet,
Tied up in cloth, big as my two hands.
She bent down and picked it up,
Then held it in both her hands.
And with that budget she rose straight up
Into the oak tree limbs and was gone.

Then crickets called, and tree frogs,
And the wind shook rustling in the trees.

I rode on to find Gabe, who said
I was white as a bedsheet in the moon.

Jim and the Ghost

That was back when I was courting Mandy Hoskins. She lived over there at Maples Creek. I used to walk over there in the evening, when plowing was done—walk back about midnight. 'Course I had to pass Mount Comfort and the cemetery there going and a-coming. Didn't bother me none. People did say it was hainted. One time Aunt Marthy King—she lived there in sight of the graveyard then—said they was some drunkards coming home from the saloon in Buena. They went out in the grave yard to where Old Jane Parish is buried. "Sleep on Jane Parish," they commence to yelling, "Sleep on till the Judgement Day." Well, when they said that, they was a light come up out of Jane Parish's grave—Aunt Marthy said she seed it—it was brighter an' the moon and 'bout as big as your two hands. Went right up over their heads.

Well, come along Revival time and me and Mandy was getting right thick. I was a-going nearly every night. Well, during the Revival they was some mean boys got to scaring folks. There was Gabe Hallmark, Wes McAuley, and Simeon Roberts' oldest boy—can't think of his name—they'd one of them wrap hisself up in a bedsheet and roll out from behind the bushes, down the hill from the graveyard. People'd be leaving the Revival, going home by the graveyard and there'd be this white thing come a rolling down at 'em. Scared some folk right bad.

'Course I didn't have to go courting during the Revival—Mandy's folks was big Baptists and they all was there every night, so I'd just meet her at the church and we could talk all we wanted to there on a back seat. Well, last day of the Revival, Gabe Hallmark come up to me, says, "Jim," he says, "I reckon you'd better no be a-going by the graveyard of a night, cause they's lots of folks seen a haint there, come a rolling down at 'em." I knowed what he was up to, so I patted on my coat pocket, and I says, "I reckon there's any haint comes rolling down that hill at me, he'll get filled full of lead." And I patted my coat pocket again. He knowed what I meant. Warn't never no ghost bothered me.

Lillie Loreen

We named her Lillie Loreen—Lillie after Pa's sister, but we called her Digs 'cause of the way she walked, her toes diggin' in the ground.

We thought she was going to die that first winter. The deathwatches ticked in the wall and there was a mourning noise under the house; we thought it was a sign, but come to look, it was just dogs fightin'.

Then spring come and Digs got well. One day she run in the house with mud on her hands and left a handprint on the screendoor there. That summer we put her out in the sunshine with Little Roy and had her picture made. Diggs pulled up the blanket in her mouth just as they made the picture—that's the only picture we have of her.

When Christmas come, Opp give us a hoop of cheese out of the store. Little Digs never had had any before and she ate so much it give her the colic. They called Dr. Massey from Buena, but he couldn't do nothing.

When we moved away from there, we throwed the broom back in the house because it's bad luck to move a broom. But we took down the screendoor and moved it with us—there's the print of her hand on it in mud.

Jim Towns' Funeral

Lon Webb's first wife was a McRea, then he married a Williams, Squirrel Hunting Billy Williams' oldest daughter—mother was a Hudson from over in Benton County. Well, their girl had a baby by Joel Towns and that was Jim, only he went by Williams and he married Gyp Collins' wife after Gyp died—mule run away with him over by Old Nineveh—that one-eyed mule Gyp bought from Turner Jones when he lived at the Roberts' place 'fore old Ike died. After she left him and took up with Dade Flowers, he married Old Bony Hawkins' girl—one that had the bastard by Ambrose Gywnn only it died of the measles—Sadie Tubbs brought 'em in to their house when her oldest girl—what was her name? I always called her Lou but that weren't her name, a tall girl, never did get married that I know of—had 'em. Well, after she died he married Dicey McCollum's sister, Lydie was her name—named after Aunt Lyde Gooch that was Sion Gooch's wife. Sion was the one that killed Henry Autry in a fight. Law never did do nothing with him about that. Sheriff was his brother-in-law.

Well, Lydie was his last wife, poor old thing. I's there when he died, setting up with him. Died of painter's colic. Didn't drink enough whisky in time to kill the poison. Aunt Lydie kept a-saying, "Give him some sweet milk, that'll help him, give him some sweet milk." Heh, he's dead and we had him laid out on a door shutter set up there on two straight chairs. Made me feel plum queer, that old woman talking like that—'course she's out of her head by then, had been for a long time. She'd go up to him and just rub his face and say, "Give him some sweet milk, that'll help him."

Well, Corbit Jones come the next day from Buena and made his coffin—he's the one had them blind children, there was four of them—I used to go with Ida. By then he'd drawed up in a knot. Well, we had to get some baleing wire and tie him down in the coffin so he'd look decent. Cal Williams was there—that was his brother—actually it was his half brother's boy. Cal weren't worth shooting and I reckon that Jim weren't no better, eemb if he is dead. Some of the McCollum relations, I don't remember which one, Jacob and Dicey had a yard full of kids, brought some baked sweet 'taters. So Cal he goes in the kitchen, gets a sweet 'tater, slips it in Jim's hand—reckon he thought that was funny, him laying there in his coffin like he was eating a sweet 'tater. 'Course we'se all setting around talking, and didn't no body notice it. He kept a-drawing up and drawing up as he got cold and long about midnight he drawed up till them wires broke that was up over his breast and he set up in his coffin a-holding a baked sweet 'tater—I reckon that room did empty.

To Tell My Tale

I stop and breathe for an undone life.
Dust in a double-handful speaks.

He had a marble field there in the yard
            Where the grass hasn't grown yet.
        He came in the back door one day
And told his mother to put his marbles up,
                He didn't feel like playing.
    He was retarded
            From brain-fever, and blind in one eye;
He was eleven when what of his life there was
Came to an end.

        Grandpa kept his marbles
In a tobacco pouch, his fishhooks
Stuck down into a corn-cob
Wrapped round with the line.
        And I have kept them.

        He was the lost boy
That grandfather in his eighties
Wandered off, hunting for,
And could not remember his name.
Roy was his name.

Roy was the name
Grandpa sometimes called me
When I was little.

I tell you this
Because the memories cry out
Like new widows in the night.
                    I tell you this,
               Burning the hours of my life
For lives lived
Because they were
      Too short
Cramped and diseased and blind and weak-minded.

I tell you this because my chin is pointed,
My hair red-brown,
      Just like Roy's.

Trojan in Carroll County

That was before Lindie married—we was coming back from a play-party at Dicey Hallmark's, me and Opp and Lindie; it was over on that hill past Kit Roberts' old place, there with all them cedar trees where there used to be a mule lot. It was setting side of the road there where there was a open field. I remember it looked like a man only it was all covered with hair, red-brown, like a horse, only it was long and shaggy—I couldn't see it well enough to tell, but that's what Lindie told me. Opp thought it was a bear, but it wadn't no bear. I can remember seeing the moon in its eyes—it was a bright moonshiney night, and you could just see the moon shining off its eyes and it followed us with its eyes when we walked passed it. We'se all scared, but wadn't nothing to do but we must go past it, it was 'tween us and home. I remember them eyes following me with the moon in 'em. Didn't move nor nothing, just stood there, big and dark, a-watching us. Well, Lindie was the only one that could see good, so we put her in the middle, with me and Opp on either side and she turned around backwards so she could see if it was coming after us. She could walk that way, me holding one of her arms and Opp the other one, and we walked as hard as we could and it didn't follow us nor nothing.

Levi Butler

Levi was kicking in my belly when I got a letter
I could not read. Lizzie Jones come and read it for me.
It said I was a widow. I cannot remember
How bitter the next four weeks were,
But I tell you that the pain of that birthing
Was sweet relief to me, and sweeter still
That I held a boy in my arms
And named him for my father.

Wild he grew without a man, and I knew
That I was born for grief and he
Was born for worse than grief.

Hard those years and bitter,
Bitter scrabbling to feed my son,
More bitter yet to see him steal
And lie and drink and fight.
But I wore out and died and God in mercy
Spared me the rest of Levi's life.

I.
LEVI'S FIRST THEFT

I stole a limb off of Jerry Garrett's tree
And then his daughter, after that, Delia.

One moony night I crossed his field
With no sound but the groaning
Of his mill; no sound except

My broughans crushing
Now and then, one damp clod.
No fear—for all his promised vengeance
We was too good to kill a man
For that. Up in front
A row of blackness, blacker than the sky
The moon had weeded of stars—his pine tree row,
Shoots brought in from Cincinnati with the mail,
Coasting dollars, at Westport train stop.

The branches snapped, scented the air
With a sweet smell of stealing—for the scent I came
For my mother to pack in with my Sunday clothes.
The sound of the limbs as they broke
And the long thin needles whispering on the air,
Woke a dog to bark. I heard
A bullet whiz by my head
And the bang of the gun.
　　　Beyond the trees, by the road
Arvil Walters was shooting at me.
Or over me. He never came
Closer than to whisper in my ear "You'll live!
"You'll live!" bullet by bullet as they passed.

It was running down that hill, falling in the gully
That nearly killed me, and I think
It was the sound of Arvil laughing there behind me
　　　　That finally killed him.
　　　　　　Or that I got no branches
Or that I got that girl in the deal
Got Delia, got in spite of Arvil.
Killed him.

II.
LEVI'S SONG

I dreamed that Delia Garrett came
And stood above my bed
Which was my coffin in the dream,
Although I was not dead.

She took her small white hands and tore
My linen shirt apart
And reached into my hairy chest,
Pulled out my beating heart.

She held it steaming, dripping there
As any bad child might
A fledgling bird found on the ground
Between its death or flight.

They buried me and walked away
And left me drowning there
In earth's great sea without a light
Or friend or breath of air.

While Delia held my heart above
A bitter, smoking fire
That filled my coffin with the reek
And snap of burning briar.

With steam of heart blood choking blind
I tore the coffin lace,
Needing Delia Garrett as
Sunlight and air and space.

Sweating, I woke up safe in bed.
And swore upon my life
By the bloody sun that rose in the east
Delia would be my wife.

DELIA EXPLAINS

Ma kept to her bed
The last ten years she lived, so I
Was woman of the house, and Ulan
Was more a son to me than brother.

We lived quiet, and the going
Of the days we heard no more
Than the mill that clanked
And splattered without stop.

When Ulan died it was as though
The mill and all had stopped
And the world came quiet
As the stars burning a-night.

Then Levi Bolton walked up the path
Singing some vulgar song,
Loud and too much alive.
And Pa turned and saw him.

And I saw him too, and after that
There was nothing for it
But I must marry that wild man
For Pa's sake. Yes, and for mine.

III.

LEVI'S WEDDING

Shouting and shooting and drinking—
And it was all from Jerry Garrett's purse
As though his silver dollars that had soured so long
        In that black withered pouch, let out
Had spread out wings bright proud and wild.

My wedding—or
To tell a truth bitter as quinine
That cures the summer chills—Delia's,
Jerry's girl he let me have
For fear she might ruin on the shelf,
Like meal that sits in his mill too long.

I danced with Delia first, and then
Her father, brothers took her
Round the sanded floor, and I laughed
Like blind Opp's fiddle,
Prattling "Soldier's Joy"—
Till sudden my laughing clabbered
Sour as milk that sits in summer,
For Arval Walters swung into her arms
And she moved her body with his body
To the music of that blind-eyed man,
Who could not see what they did
But rubbed his bow, commanding them
To move like lust.

        Gone in a minute—
But I was cold in my sweat, needing

To fill the balance, sure as the meal
Jerry Garrett weighs out. Ella Roland
Stood as close as my long arms' reach,
Blue and cool as the mill pond frozen
When I sawed blocks for the icehouse out.

What shall I say? I dove
Deeper than I dared into
Green cool eyes, danced a round
With Ella holding to one side
Her blue and lacy skirt.

The night grew wobbly on its feet, Opp, tired
Let the bow drag on the strings, feet scraped
The sanded floor, the old folks
Clattered off in their wagons. I went
With my woman to do
In the dark what animals do.

IV.
LEVI'S BUILDING

"Measure twice, cut once"—I'm good
At what I put my hand to; no other way
Could I have bought out Jerry Garrett,
Millstones and store and all.

To marriage I put my hand—
Swore an oath and wrote
In a Preacher's book.
        It would have been
True as an angle

Marked with a T-square,
    It would have held
Tight as a board nailed straight in.

But it was not.

I ask my hands
What went wrong,
While I build this house
For my second woman.

           Delia's up there
           In the big house I built
           To last a life—for us.

I reckon she hears my hammer.
I reckon every knock on the nail
Is like a nail in her coffin.

Delia, my wife, from whose body
I've harvested a son and a daughter.

I swear I love her true as this saw
Cuts out the pencil line.
    No fault
With her flesh in the dark, no grief
For her cooking, sewing, behavior
In public places.

But the wood
Splits as it will.

Ella Roland tangled me
In her eyes.
      And I
Was too glad to throw
Those knots about me.

Can there be
Two right angles not true
To one another? There's one
To ask Opp who figures in his head.

I had to have Ella.
Loved Ella as I love
The wife I'm tied to
Flesh and soul and name and all.

So I'm building a house to keep her in
      Down the road from the first house I built.
        The note of the hammer on the nail
Rings more shrill as it dives straight in.
        Angle by angle, perfect, measured,
Set to last
As long as it must.

v.

ULAN

Delia's Young Brother

I was a red sun rising, the birds
Whistled a glad jangling—then sudden the dark.
I grew to be almost a man among old men
Who could be spared to go to mill,

To spit and talk while rock on rock
Ground out the fresh warm meal.
When I had come to sixteen years my father hired
Levi Butler to work at the mill,
And my life opened out broad wings and flew.
He took me with him after work
To bars in Westport town, where lights
Burned all the night and the women
Were painted and sang
Of the sweet pain of love, of the desirable grief
Of loving which I did not know.
He passed the jug of liquor that had fire
Smoky and smoldering in it while we sat,
Levi and I, beside a hunting fire,
And watched the 'possum we had treed
Spit and brown over the fire.
Oh, and life burned in me, a fire in my chest,
As though I ran too fast, too far,
Life that had opened so sudden
          Like a summer sunrise, like a quick fire
      Built in the woods. Dr. Compton called that fire
              Tuberculosis. One night past midnight
Levi and I rode home from the women and the wine
In a pouring winter rain. The cold
Went into my bones. My sister Delia stripped me,
Dried me, not minding my nakedness, put me to bed.
I never left that bed alive, but after two days
Talking of painted women and the fire
My ribcage held like a stove, I went
And chased the sunset out of sight.

VI.

LEVI'S KILLING

I'd shoot a thief
In my corn crib—who wouldn't?
Jerry Garrett—no, he'd let
Thieves strip his pine trees till they bled
Their lives out in golden rosin. Jerry
Never shot me, though I stole him blind
And bought his mill with his gold and married
His white virgin daughter.

I'm not Jerry Garrett to let a man
Take what's mine although
I never put my name on her.

                Fed her at my hand—caught Ella
                Sure as a hunter catches a crow,
Teaches it to speak his name.

I'm Levi Butler, if you want my name.
Delia is my wife and Ella Roland's
Something of mine too, and sure as hell
She was not for Arvil Walters.

I swear
I never heard the gun go off.
It was as though my hatred killed that man,
With no gun or other ugly thing
Between my pure clear soul and his
Soft blood-filled flesh.

He simply curled and died there
On the dusty moonlit road
From Dollar to Garrett's Mill.

VII.

DELIA TELLS WHAT MATTERS

Do I care what he does? No more
Than I care how our dogs
Couple in the yard. Those tears
Dried long ago. When he took
That whore it only left me
                    With less to put up with
                    From him in the night. I sing
                    Around the kitchen with my children
And Levi Butler climbs on whom he will,
                    Shoots, for what I care,
Any fool that grazes in his field.

Yes, I saw that Arvil Walters
Coming and going where he'd better not.
And yes, Levi left my bed
The night that Arvil was shot.

What matters to me
Is the sunlight that fills my kitchen
In the morning, and teaching Clara
To talk and sing while Joney
Scribbles his letters on kindling wood
And sounds out words for me.

VIII.

JONEY REMEMBERS

I remember her as kind,
That other woman who was not
My mother, she that my mother
Told us not to say
One word to, although
She gave us candy bought
At Martin Butler's store.
Pappy's friend, but none
Of Mammy's—I didn't know
How that could be. She lived
Just up the road and Pa
Went there and stayed sometimes,
And mammy cried for missing him,
So I asked if I shouldn't go
Up there and bring him home,
For I was old enough to walk
That far alone. At that
She stopped crying and from that day
I never saw her cry again,
Though there were many nights
When Pa was never home.
Instead she sat with me
And taught me books, and pulled
The blinds down on that side
The house. She didn't even cry
The day they put
Her husband in the ground.

IX.

LEVI'S DEATH

Three views on the event

i. A Neighbor

'Course I knew he'd die like that
Or worse. Don't no man do
What he had done and expect
To die in bed with grandchildren
Crying round him like the angels.

Got it sudden in his barn
Feeding his dapple mare—if the County
Finds the man that shot him
Neat in the heart by the light
Of the new risen sun, I think
We owe that man pure money
For doing what the law
Needed to have done long ago.

Ain't nobody knows Levi don't know who
　　Killed Arvil Walters and why. Nor nobody either
　　But thinks they both got what they needed.
And that's all I'll say.

ii. Delia, His Wife

　　　　　　It's been too quiet here
Since I heard that gunshot and dropped
A fist of biscuit dough that would never be
My husband's breakfast.
　　　　　　Joney went to run

Out to the barn, but I held him back
With a floury hand on his homespun shirt.
No need for the boy ever to remember
That bloody sunrise and his father
Dead among the horses there.

Ella's gone
A-whoring in another place.
Levi's stiff and cold
And in hell I guess.
He and Arvil Walters
Boast to each other
Of the women they rode
While clawing in the fire.

And I the widow
Sing around my kitchen
When the sun comes gold and scarlet
Up the sky and Clara sings with me,
And Joney reads the Bible to me
And remembers no blood.

iii. Clara, His Daughter

Papa killed a man and a man killed papa
That's all the song I know
Papa killed a man and a man killed papa
Sung to any tune, that's the way it'll go.

If you ask me at church,
If you ask me at school
Which 'un was wise
Which 'un was a fool—

Papa killed a man and a man killed papa.
Maybe cause he slept with a whore—
Papa killed a man and a man killed papa
That's all there is, there ain't no more.

A 'Possum Tale

One time ol' Jim Towns killed him a 'possum—found it eatin' 'simmons in the tree after the leaves had fell—warn't no big 'possum, hardly enough fat on it to cook it. Well, Jim, he took him a Model T tire pump and stuck the hose up in that 'possum's ass and pumped it up till it looked plum fat. Jim, he had that pumped up 'possum a-laying out on a stump in front of his house when Uncle Ben McAuley he come along. He stopped, come up on the porch and they's talking. "Mighty pretty 'possum you got out there," Uncle Ben says. "Yeah," Jim says. "I been a-eating 'possums here for a week till I'se tired of 'em. Don't reckon I could stand another one of 'em. Let me sell you that fat 'possum." "Well," says Uncle Ben, "I ain't got nothing but this here jug of moonshine." Jim, he picked up that jug and shook it and it was plum nearly full. "A deal," he says and shook hands on it. Well, soon as Uncle Ben picked up that 'possum he noticed it was mighty light. Got home with it he stuck a knife in it, commencing to skin it and that let the air out—weren't nothing but the boniest old 'possum you ever seed. Then when Jim tried to drink that moonshine, found out it was the hottest old pop-skull you ever tasted—warn't fittin' to drink nor nothin'.

Nate and Cindy

PROLOGUE
Tell the story: a love story;
Tender touched the lovers, proper as spring;
But death was the ending of it.
    For loving,
Oh, for weeping in secret and longing
When the fat red sun
Lumbered to rest,
For the caring and the dreaming,
Standing with his hoe
In the weedy corn.

For that
Death.

Because he whispered to her
The common secrets of an honest heart,
Death, because his finger
Traced words he could not write upon her cheek, death,
Death for caring, hoping, death—for the dance of love
The dance in the noose.

For this reason:
That she was white, he black.

1.
There was an old beech tree
That grew beside a spring.

Flints in the black earth said that Indians
Had hunted there; passed ghosts there
Searching for a land not to be taken away.

    Two grown men
Could not join arms around the trunk
Of that old tree. Cindy Hallmark came
For water there and sat upon the roots
Because her mother's kitchen was so hot,
And the water curled cool
Around her feet and the water
Sang cool and the wind
Was cool in the beech leaves,
And she slept. And she woke.
And there was Nate
Looking at her.
                He seemed
Some part of the dream,
Or of the waking, some piece
Of the rest and the wind
And the singing water, Nate.
Black, stripped to the waist,
Muscular and harmless
As the smooth corded beech bark,
Nate—in his eyes, something
Of the fallen fledgling.

Nate found her dreaming
And beginning to dream himself
Found his death:

" 'Lo—I'm Nate.

We'se working over there.
Mighty hot."
                    From the dreams
Moving under her eyelids, her face
Upturned to the sky, looking
At an interior horizon, flesh only
Like still water where the sun
Does not waver; this
Is what Nate saw.

Waking from no dream
She could remember, she found
In a stripling lad
The joy of the word.

He tore a piece of string
From his old shirt, stiff with salt,
And knotted it once for every time
They met beside the spring.

The second time
Was nearly unplanned:

"Miss Cindy—I seed
You here before."

"Ma uses lots of water
A-making kraut, you know."

"I loves kraut."

"I does too,

But hit's too much trouble."

"See you tomorrow,
I reckon." Small talk
With pounding hearts; in the same place
They met again, said again
Such silly things.

Many the knots in Nate's blue string.
Hours the talks, looking
Into the sun that bounced
In the water.

Did flesh ever act out
The mixing of the heart? Danced
Your bodies into one knot?—
Mean to ask what life for them
Flowed quiet as the water,
Quiet as the moon
Through a web of stars.

II.
Cindy had a sister, a child
Like the Cherokee rose, wild and thorny
Gadding on fences. She spied and
Brought home the word:

"Cindy's boyfriend's a nigger!"

"Ain't so," said Cindy, but her nerves

Told other things. Her father
Read her fears as, probing,
He came nearer and nearer.
He shouted. She wept. He guessed,
And hit her. There was blood.
She told all—

Meeting place. Time.

Death. There was nothing but pain,
And worse than pain, his anger
Like white sheets of lightning.

Mercy of her mother weeping.
Mercy of cold silence. One cold thought
Beating like a dead crow
Hung in the garden, beats
Beats against the apple tree
In the spring wind:
"Life will not be very long."

Landrum Hallmark prayed to Christ
All that night for what to do.
Prayed, prayed while the cold stars
Moved over the face of the night
                Like some slow rain upon his face.
He prayed to God who hung on tree
Because his girl had ruined him,
Because she'd played worse than whore,
Because he'd slept with his wife
Before they said the words

This came on him.
　　　God of vengeance,
Anger, who pays with hell
All apples stolen, He
Will strengthen that failing
That falling, fumbling
In the dark to more than dark
So long ago—forgive with death
Landrum's lusting that brought down
Shame on his house—forgive
Lord Christ who hung on tree,
Sin's warning to all who steal.
Forgive with death.

He was a mild man, Landrum.
When the dawn came and the cock crew
He had decided to call another dog
To do his killing for him.
　　　　　　　　A mild man,
He kissed the bruises he'd left
On Cindy—cold, trembling
Dry from weeping, dry
To the soul as a mummy.
"Darling," was all that he said,
Leaving. His next words
Killed a man for loving his child.

For he spoke to Green McCoy
Who had ridden with Forrest, and thought
He'd lived no day so fine
As Fort Pillow when he denied

That slaves could make soldiers
By shooting them like fish in a barrel.

"Rape" was the word
That undid his shame.
"Rape" was the bait
He threw to his dog
And it burned
Like lightning in his eyes.

One pure girl
Defiled—a death
Would answer it.

III.
When the leaves are new
And perfect, the Cherokee roses
    Bloom in May, the daisies
    And the iris by the water.

By the water that prattles
Over the grey roots,
When the Cherokee rose was going,
The honeysuckle coming.

Roots of an old beech—
On that tree, on a day
That God made,
They hung Nate Simons
Whom God had died for

Without conceding so much
As a mask for their shame,
They hung Cindy's gentle lover
And left him there.

Roots of an old tree, gnarled,
Like knotted hands, praying
Into the black earth—
The whippoorwills
Sung back and forth
And the body of Nate Simons
Swung gently, slowly
In the evening breeze.

Cold and stiff the muscles,
Ready for the earth the bones
That the mid-spring morning sun
Found live and tender.

Flesh like the flowers in the fields
And the grass; heart rising up
And dancing full of birdsong,
Sunlight and Cindy. Death.

Death and hate
Fruits of an old tree.
Ghosts of Indians
Hunt the long hunt.
Dark feet move
Silent among the leaves,
Stirring no gillyflower.

Adam from that garden,
Father of all, when
Shall all the offspring of the earth
Possess that that they are?

Not that we humans are so unredeemed—someone
Came and gouged deep in grey beech bark
One simple word—"Murder."

An Angel of the Darker Wine

These angels came
Out of great hatred; they share
The silence of the dead, souls
Marbleized, flesh lepered with lichen,
Trumpet to lip to wake
The dead, they do not wake
Themselves, or any dead, but fall,
Molting in the decades, stone wing
By stone wing; a mortality
Of the immortal, roots only
Heave up from the grave, plying
At their angelic pedestals, and ice
In winter like bitter hatred
       Bears down on their translucent wings,
       That break like tree limbs, groaning
       In the dark wind: A story:

Nathan Nesbitt came and took land,
Red clay, and fertilized it with black slaves,
Set cotton by boatloads river-to-river
To ocean and grew rich.
               And died
Leaving words on paper, naming heirs
Who heirs had themselves till at the core
Of Nathan's tribe there sat
One old maid and she
Was more bitter than the gall
Of all the gold that had come to her.
She fought off nieces' love and nephews' courting

Because she heard the clink of gold,
Hunger for gold, her gold
In every word they spoke to her,
Every flower they sent to her
Touched with a mind
Cursed as Midas till it turned
To gold's cursed wanting all the milk
Of human kindness. Ashes, ashes.
And what was there left for her?
Withered maid—not the flesh,
Nor the joy of coin on coin.
Till a day came when all she needed
Of dead Nathan's coins
Was two quarters saved for her eyes.
So in her dying days she sent
The money that had come back
For cotton picked by slaves
To Italy where Carrara craftsmen carved
Angels for her into this world
That lacked angels so sore—
Chisels found vaulting wings,
And flurry of heavenly robes
Disarranged by material wind
In blocks of marble and they came sailing
The sea, a flock, an annunciation
Of seraphim, crated to light
On Nathan's grave and on all the graves
Of all who ever gave her love,
Peaceful marble from stained gold
Hammered till every cent was gone
And she could die content
That nothing was left for unworthy hands.

So now they wait in the old family plot,
Blowing their silences and crumbling
Their Judgement Day for all who see
To guess what judgement and on whom.

In a Country Churchyard

Oldest graves in the center, here;
Like a lichen on grey stone
The graves have grown outward.

Jeffrey Butler. 1963–1985
I heard about it—drag racing
Down the crooked Buena road.

What was left of him
Lived for ten minutes
      his brother said.

Here's my great-grandmother Butler
Dead now these fifty-two years. My mother
Can remember her. Peace to her;
They say she was kind.

And Uncle Jeems Butler, the miller, who kept
My family alive through the Civil War.
When women were selling themselves
To blue soldiers, to grey soldiers
For a sack of meal
Because they had children;
Uncle Jeems fed my people
And I remember it.

And near the center,
A cousin, Grey Butler.
His tombstone says he was murdered

On the day after Christmas
A hundred and twenty years ago.
My grandfather had the story
From his sister when she was
A bitter old woman. He could name
Five men, one of whom did it;
                              they all lie here.

Coarse grass only in the center
            for the pioneers.
The Cemetery Committee
Threw the uncut rocks away
That marked the oldest graves.

I remember it. May God.

I remember an old man pointing with his stick,
Naming in a broken voice
Ancestors under this rock and that.

Elias Butler is here somewhere,
Revolutionary soldier who came
To Tennessee in his eighties,
                  Moving like a patriarch in Genesis
                  With his nine children,
                  Uncounted grandchildren.
                              Gad.
      A troop cometh.

Some part of me,
      color of my hair,

shape of my hand,
bits of songs,
stories
Moved in among them.
(Teraphim, household gods.)

Spring's begun, the sunlight
Is full of unopened buds,
The quiet forest
Waits for birds.

And here in the center
peace of the dead.
No wind
Rattles a brown dry leaf, no bird
Calls out. The peace is close to me and warm.
I do not fear the silence,
God is in it.

Some other where
The young who threw away their lives,
Or had them stolen sudden from them,
The old who lived theirs out,
Are in the silence with God,
Are in the darkness that God
Informs with love.
No fear here.

The silence is peace
Darkness
Is warmed by deep light.

Peace,
I say peace,

To the kind
    To the generous
    Who gave their shelled corn to the hungry
    When there was not enough.

Peace.

            I give remembrance.

                        And
            To those who stole the rocks.
In heaven, in earth,
Remembrance also.

Natchez Trace

They gave it back, the land,
To the wildness that waited
In field corners and creek bottoms
And moved on, leaving
Bricks of a hearth
Cold in the woods.

Dead to the earth.
Fields to the woods.
Song and laughter and weeping
           To the air, to the free air.

Find them?

Daisies
Drenched in dew and sunlight—
Daisy was Luther's child
And Lindie's.

There, before it goes,
          Some word rustles
       Out of the star-shaped gum leaves—
        Pattern for a quilt, twigs
         Sweet green that I chewed
      For toothbrushes that old women
     Dipped snuff with—a word, a symbol
        Runs, free as a bubble
   and is gone.

Color of eyes—
Clear skies and dark water.

Running, glint of lightning,
Axes that felled the forest,
That did not fall, but remains
The border of all.

Shimmer of shadows
Playing in the water,
Dancing down Sandy River.

They are
Imminent, in eternity
That has returned
                    With the forest.

In a Garden

There was an apple tree
And an old woman owned it.

There were two children
Who stole apples and ran away
Laughing over their shoulders.

Poison she got, poison
And smeared it on the apples.

They took them home to their mother,
Their father and three younger children.

Seven graves there are in a row
In New Friendship Cemetery.

Marksmanship

Two bullets to kill
Two rabbits a day, one
To feed his wife and
Sons, one rabbit
To sell for the price
Of two bullets.

Lizzie's Tale

How would I know what it was. He just come and said he wanted work, with a sack over his shoulder. Jim—that was my first husband—hired him and he was a good worker. Many's the day we've worked in the fields together the three of us, and that Indian would always keep up with his row. Well, he asked Jim where he could put his sack, so Jim told him to hang it in the hen house. Ever' day when I went to get eggs I'd brush up against it, and didn't think nothing about it. It rattled. Well, he worked for us 'bout a year, and come times he was a-leaving. He went and got his sack and Jim asked him what was in it. He poured it out there on the ground and it was the bones of a man. He said he could throw the shin bones and the knucklebones and tell the future with 'em—and me rubbing by that thing ever' day!

Cu Sidh

She's seeing
Things that aren't there, now.
No brown dog crosses the yard
        To lick her hand, smooth as membrane; you can see
                        The slow dark blood
Moving around the bone.
She speaks
                To the dog we do not see,
                        Kind words.

                        She goes to live
                Among the legends she filled
Our childhoods with.
        She moves in to stay.

There'll soon be a box with a thin body in it,
A little more earth for the great earth.

Cousin Peter

A rough young farmer, unpracticed
At weeping, his calloused hands
Hurt his eyes, he sobs
Like an animal, like a goat
Trussed up for its throat to be slit,

Still a human weeping.

In a ladder-backed chair,
Under a beech tree,
Initials blurring in its bark
Like the rings on a turtle's shell.

Behind him an empty house,
An empty home, a dead young wife,
An only son dead.

In front of him a fire,
         One by one, page by page,
         Fed with love letters
         From a hand where the pulse
          Has stopped. The fire
           Glows brighter
          Page by page.

Above him the trees
Burgeoning into leaf.

When the leaves are the size

Of a squirrel's ear,
Corn ought to be planted.

Around him his fields
Still in grey, rotting stubble.

And from somewhere within,
Life calls to him with a horrible voice.

He will remarry.

Oliver Grogan

Oliver Grogan—you know Oliver—he was raised over there by Clyde Parish's old place. Make a left there at the road turns off past Gus Grissom's place. Gus was a piano tuner and organ fixer—told me one time he thought about killing hisself, got out his razor and make a mark 'round his throat with it where he would cut. Well, that hurt so bad he decided he wouldn't do it. Then you take a left, cross the Sandy there at the Little Bridge, and Mart—that was Oliver's father, lives about a mile beyond that—well, anyhow, Oliver Grogan was in World War One—went over there to France. Said they don't talk like we does—couldn't understand nobody. It was just like a turkey gobbling—I've heard him do it—he learned some of their talk. You've heard of Joan of Arc? Oliver said he saw the stump she used to stand on and preach—right out there in the field, she was a woman, but she used to preach he said. Must 'a been a Holiness. Well, he come back home, it was in April, and we'd had a month of rain. Sandy River was up—whole bottom was flooded. Oliver, he come in to Buena on the train. Got to Dollar—he was a walking—they told him in the store, said, "You'll have to stay here a few days, 'cause the road to you Pa's place is flooded." "Heck," says Oliver, "I done come over a bigger piece of water 'an the Sandy River." Sure enough, he swum that river, got home in time for supper.

Winter of 1941

A car whipped her legs with her skirt
On the narrow shoulder of the Roosevelt Road
On the causeway where the man had been put under
Four years before, killed in a knife fight.

Then the car was gone up Dollar Hill
And there was no sound or brightness
In the winter world except the polished oaken case
Of the Silvertone Radio she was taking home.

It was big as a cradle and heavy
As though it were full of chains
And she had bought it with her brother's Navy money
So she could hear the news of World War II.

The winter of '38 they lived on potatoes
And credit until Dick lied
About his age and her mother
Wept and signed the enlistment paper.

The world had been, longer than anyone remembered,
Fields and woods and sleepy rivers, and the dance
Of seasons demanding planting, harvest
And generations coming, going, all, always, at once.

But the green and golden ring where they
Had suffered with all before them was pierced now
With roads and electricity and war
And a change colder than the wind.

Cousin Loney

Her Bible's on the second shelf, kept
     behind the stove,
     under a vine.

Plants everywhere
In tubs and pots
And tea kettles that leaked.

Smell of roses in January.

Five lines
Written by a hand
That knew the hoe better
Sum up her life:

Married.
Sons born.
Husband dead.
Son killed.
     Near Rome, 1944.

It was the thin fighting
When Mussolini was hanging by his heels
Like a pig
On a gamlin stick.

     Her lead-grey hair tight in a bun,
     She sings old love-songs as she waters
     Cacti planted in sand,

Mums with bitter smelling leaves.

A stray bullet in a campaign that was over.

Her remaining son comes in
Drooling, feeble-minded.

Flowers kept through the winter,
     outside
Powder of snow on the frozen ground.

III

BREAKING—A NEW WORLD

Snow

There was snow.

       That is the oldest memory.

          I was a child
      In arms and some adult
Held me up to a window and said "Look."

I was weeping,
I had seen
My grandmother in her coffin;
"Look! The snow" to stop my crying.

Her face was still and pale—
Cold, very cold.

It was a new thing.
"Say 'snow'" but I knew
What death was
     just not the word.

This is the start of the book
That I remember,
     a dead face
Below me, that I had loved
Better than the world.

There was a black tree,
Negative lightning,

Standing up from the earth.
      The voice and the arms
That held me said it would soon bear fruit,
Red fruit. "Strawberries?" I asked
Through gulps of air, knowing
No other fruit.
      "Cherries,"
I think they said,
                   But I did not stop.

                   Dead love
Stands at the start of the book
And makes all the lyrics elegies.

See the pretty world child
And stop crying.

It never worked.

Purple

They say that grandmother planted it.
I remember that no more
Than I remember
The knobbed hands that held me,
Her first-born grandchild, helpless
As a seedling and wailing purple.

I suppose she saw her daughter
Had no love for her stray
Mistake of a child.
She died just one spring later,
Too soon to fill my childhood
With any love;

Only to leave me a lilac
With her fingerprints among its roots—
A sweet purple Eden each spring.

Going Home

The wind in the pine trees is lonelier than I can stand;
It wants my arm on its shoulder, my tears
Mixed forever in the rain. I will go back.

The mountains' gesture on the horizon undoes me,
As though their proud stone hearts unsaid
The "be thou" of God that is me. And when I think
The words the pine trees find in the wind will wear
        down
The face of the mountains
Watched by the merry stars, then my time,
With a love or without, is nothing. I will go back.

Back to rooms where there are ticking clocks,
And friends, and tea on Friday afternoons.

The desolate graves in the woods,
Marked with uncut stones, where all my fathers sleep
Tell me in the nights that the lichens
Are gnawing at my name.
And in the country churches beside them,
Old men with broken voices
Sing like wagons rolling on stony ground,
And, the word is not worship,
But dread, God of Calvin,
Who makes me doubt
If all my love could move one mote,
Eternal as a star sinking in the sunrise. I must go back.
To the miles of silent bookshelves,

And the streetlights that dome the city with glare
Safe from the killing hail
Of blue, eternal stars.

Picnic on the Fourth

No fooling the country eye; they know
How lost I am here
In the county where I grew up—my staring
At the line of trees that rings
Our world with the primeval
Tells them that. I heard
Some far-off music; mine
About this world where I am
Both so much at home and so much
A stranger in a strange land.

Otis is a pilot star to me;
We were boys together, our leg bones
Grew long the same time,
Running these fields, bruising
The sweet scent of broomsedge, burning
Our lungs with panting and laugher.
That is our friendship—
The bass continuo of those lost summers.
His plain sweet wife teems with children
From ten-year-olds to three-,
But where are mine . . . ?

Otis asked to say grace
Stumbles through a remembering
Of our many blessings, and commemorates
The founding fathers who bequeathed us liberty.

I think of my ancestor from North Carolina

Who fought in the Revolution,
And came to Tennessee in his eighties
To die. They say the fighting in the Carolinas
Was mean and personal, no pitched battles in clean uniforms,
But guerilla-style like Vietnam
        Browne at Augusta,
        Banastre at Cloud Creek—
I stumble along with Otis
In my trying to bless—Vietnam
Where we killed children and lost?

In the hush that followed the prayer,
One sighed word of the summer wind
In the pine trees over our heads—
Pines that wake the winter
Knowing the sharp stars
That frost the frozen black,
Trees that nurse
Snow in their green arms,
Chanting that word as it melts,
Pine trees that have no spring.

Then we ate. The young marrieds
Alone in the crowd, and Otis' youngest boy
Crying till he can find his father
To eat beside. His wailing
For awhile was the only sound
Except the pine trees' monosyllable.

I fear for him—
It is also hope.

We adjourned to the pasture woods to swim
Where sunlight spreads bracken on the wet soil.
        The old folks on the way
    Remembering a lost swimming hole
Somewhere upstream.
            And I was there.
Having forgotten to bring my trunks,
I sat and turned the mills that grind
All this into poetry. Around us, above us,
The oaks have their word in the hot summer wind.

What word, what word from these trees
Whose roots mingle in the sandy clay
With the chipped arrowheads of the forgotten Indians,
Adena points, six, seven thousand-year-old,
Older than Ussher's Bible has the world,
Points the size and shape of a beech leaf for killing
birds,
Larger ones for deer, bear, men, but which
The earth has forgotten; long ago
The bones dissolved in the acid soil.

The waters that run forever are muddied
With the children fighting
For a red soccer ball brought in lieu
Of a beach ball by their dad.
It augurs ill, this fighting,
It colors my reading
Of the word on the wind.

Upstream there was indeed another swimming hole

Where another generation splashed and was cold for a while
Under July sun. While the old folks remember
Their childhoods in the twenties and thirties,
I think of Julius Caesar who gave his name to the month
Three thousand years after the Adena Indians
Came here and left their beech-leaf
Points in the soil,
And no more to remember.

Some child—was it Otis' sad little son—
Throws the soccer ball to me,
To Hamlet, and I make it Yorick's skull,
Speak a speech trippingly on the tongue
To the ball and to the uncomprehending delighted children.

And smelt so i' the earth
Pah!—the ball to a laughing girl.
Oh, life, oh, death.

As we leave the grove, an oak gall catches my eye,
Mistaken for a bird's skull—
Ink ball the old folks called it
And made ink from it; from just this
Dante's ink was made, but ground too
From the flaming cinnabar of hell,
From the opalescent moonstone of Paradise—
Fifth stone in the Apocalyptic foundations of Heaven.

Heaven a city always bothered me.
If God gives me my own Heaven
It'd be much like this

With friends and old folks
And children growing up,
But peacefully.
Perhaps to remember some lines from Hamlet.
But with trees that speak
Never darkly of death or time,
Or old bones lost in the dark
Whereon we tread.

Strangers in the Ruins

A rich man's toy farm kept
Like a boat in a bottle,
Like the spinning wheel in the parlor,
Plow in the front yard,
Calluses on no fingers.
     It was real once.
This little house
That a student rents to keep
The rain off his books and his sleep
Was home once to a farmer before Vanderbilt was built.

He invites me in and offers me
Bread and cheese and friendship,
In this renter house with old, little windows
That hobble the sun, no door
Fitting snug in its frame.
What can he make
Of the South, my city friend
From Albuquerque,
     a generic place somewhere to the dry west.

In the pasture the grass is still green;
Black Angus are grazing,
Their tails to the northwest wind,
Square, fat cows meant only for steak.

He asks me what hay is.
I smile and tell him,

But I never bent my back to the shocks,
Or sang a harvest song to the dead old year.

       Water, where it runs, has worn
    The gravel round with its song, finding
     The limestone left by a prehistoric sea.
       (There are ghosts in the stone.)

The sound of the stream holds us
Like three-year-old children to a tale
That goes on longer than it has gone.

The owner has made the barn
       into a rumpus room,
Brought in antique school desks for seats.
Children studied at these desks once,
Learned to spell and cast up accounts.

A sorghum mill
Rots to the brink of anonymity
But I know what it was, what it did;
I know from my grandfather
Who made my childhood
Bearable with talk of his good old days.
The wooden mounting is rotting away,
The wood that remains
Is moused over with green moss—
       The fingerprints of the sun
      Are caught as life, as the thin film
Between the sky and the black earth.

The chimney is gone, a piece of plywood
Covers the grief of its falling.
A rose bush is still green
Though leafless by the old brick porch.

      He thinks me displeased with this place;
        My silence and my staring trouble him.
I can't explain that this poem is growing in me;
Can't tell him yet how many layers
Of land and time and men and things
I'm staring through, probing,
Loving in my way.

We talked of beauty
When the bread and the coffee and the cheese
Were in us and thawing
More than the north wind could freeze.

"Beauty," I said,
Like the scholar it does not suit me to be,
"Beauty is a function of alienation. The old farmer,
      Whose ghost walked his fields beside us,
  Knew it as a book-word; this land was not beautiful to
                    him.
His children got the word from Longfellow's books,
And your landlord thinks a horse-drawn plow
Mounted in his yard is beautiful—
He never followed behind more
Than stock quotations."

The old farmer bargained life and peace

Out of this thin limestone soil; to him
The sunset was beautiful since it meant rest.
Now his resting place keeps the grey rain
Off your books, while you live
The student's tentative life
In a rich man's antique curio.

He loves the country imagined, I
Love the scenery of an old lore.
We both find peace here for we were both
Thrown out of Eden. The farmer's wife
Planted so a rose in her yard.

Leaving Nashville

The cotton's in the square
Under the white fire of August,
Month of preludes.
      When will the snow
Hang on the hairs of my hand
The sun has bleached white?

Corn hardens
In the shuck.

Weeds run to seed.

Leaves waste off the trees.
It's done, it's finished

It's ripe or lost or botched
Or anything
      —But over
And begun again.

On a Weed-Grown Hill

The old Bawcomb place was here, see
There's a piece of Blue Willow cup
That was made in Austria
By somebody. Eveline Bawcomb drank out of that
When she was alive.

IV

THE LOST FATHER

PREFACE

Hosea Attaway married Betty Lasiter,
Their daughter Clara married Linn Allen
Linn and Clara's son, Bill Allen
Married Hazel Jones, daughter of Jim Jones
Jim's sister was Aunt Ida. I am the son
Of Hazel Jones, and of Bill Allen
Whom I never knew.

Allen—when I say the name
To strangers, they ask again. The Ls
Drool out my mouth, soft and muddy.
It's not an old name. I never heard
My father say it. Nor he his, hardly.

Clara

Her mother was the second wife, the second chance
For Hosea Attaway who had made a family,
     got son and daughters
And seen them married off and lost a wife
     and buried her
With a still-born infant in her arms.
  A thin,
Frail girl this Betty Lasiter, she gave him three
     daughters more
While his hair turned white, gave him pratlings around
The house where the quiet had become too much.
     What was it?
Did that young wife give birth the charmed third time
To a wildness she never spoke of, never acted on
But sat and peeled apples on the porch?
  Clara ran with men
From the day her breasts began to grow—that
  Was the coughing that killed her mother, the cancer
     That ate her father's chest out. At fourteen
    She was pregnant, and afterwards she married
Linn Allen who may have been the father
And Bill was the name of that son.

With women he had neither luck nor the strength
To leave them alone. And now I cannot count
The women that he had nor the children he scattered
A boy's seed over three states
Or maybe four.
  Linn got tired

Of the children that peeped to him
　　　Like naked birds in the nest when he came home
　　From the barbershop or the factory in Jackson, so one day
He did not come home. Thirty years later
They heard of him in California, with nine
More children there. And a legend that floats
About to finish the tale has him hanging himself
Somewhere, sometime, Atlanta? Arkansas?

Bill could not stand the redneck fool
His mother married after she guessed
Her husband was dead or might as well be.
He would not share the house with this new man,
Lean as a skinned squirrel, smooth and edgy
And bitter as a snake, so he left
The red-clay hill of the hungry mouths
To live with his aunt in Jackson,
So grew up a city boy.

꙾

I remember one time while he was living with us, him and me
was just like brother and sister, but we was cousins you see—
went to the same school too. Bill couldn't spell worth nothing.
Well he was 'bout seventeen, just 'fore he joined the C.C.C. a-
building houses for Roosevelt. He knocked on the door one
night and there was Bill with one leg in his pants and one leg
out and he run through the house and right out the back door
letting the screen slam and all he says was, "The police is after
me. Don't tell 'e I'm here. It's about a woman."

꙾

Althie Nell was his first wife,
He said, it was Jack, the man
Who ruined his first marriage,
He said he and Bill
Used to ride to Crossroads church
                    In a wagon together
                    When they were boys.

It was Jack I learned later who stepped
In between Althie Nell and Bill,
Taking Althie Nell, making my father
A cuckold, and I was sitting
Talking to this whitehaired old man
With a heavy face
Who'd ruined that first marriage,
Going where he did not belong,
Another man's place,
And sent Bill roaming first,
In those wanderings that made me.

He gave me her picture, Glenn,
    The brother whom I met and loved and who died.
        Althie Nell was a woman wearing out
When somebody aimed a small camera at her
And took this one picture. It was not the face
Of that first wedding night, but a woman
Who'd sinned and been sorry for it,
And gotten over being sorry and went on
Making her life with her worn,
Bony hands.
        His mother,

Not mine, Glenn, the brother
Who was too decent to talk about
The family, said just
That he didn't know. Glenn who smoked
And ate barbecue with a gusto like mine—

ꤷ

Daddy was in the barbecue business when him and Mammy
married and they say that there weren't no better barbecue in
Henderson county than the Allen Barbecue there in Crossroads,
and that's how the Allen Food Company got started—

That must have been about the time
That Jack came into the picture—

You can ask ol' Nate Henlaw, he's a nigger, but he'll tell you,
he worked for daddy back then. Niggers is O.K., I've worked
with a many a nigger and they's as good as any body else. Now
daddy, he didn't like no niggers—Oh no, didn't like 'e a-tall.
When he had that little mechanic shop there in Tater Town,
there's a nigger come in, brought his truck in to be fixed, said
he'd pay just as soon as it was finished. He come to get it, and
told him he'd pay for it some day when he had the money.
Well, daddy, he just cold-cocked that nigger, laid him right out
there on the sidewalk in front of Allen's garage.

That must have been when he was living with Dellie
Who was the fourth wife, I think.

ꤷ

What was it, that temper,
Blinding rage, that ruined his life
Again and again?
    I ask, but I know,
Know as near to home as my own heart,
My father's heart, that feels
A fury that no power, under God,
Could fill up the wrath of.

Frustration, call it frustration.
Not fists, not tire irons,
Not guns can make
My enemy acknowledge his mistake.
I feel before the will
Of another, instead
Of my own powerlessness,
My anger—else how small,
Ineffectual might I feel?
Among the atoms I might fall away—
As though
To reach
My will
Out through my fist
To that other,
That is not my will.

That is the curse of the Allens
And of the human race.

"You wanna bring another man in over your children?"

"Mama, we gotta have somebody to take care of us."

"Your daddy'll feed you just as long as he can. And you know I'd take the last crust a' bread out a' my mouth and give it to you."

"Daddy ain't gonna live forever, you know that, Mama."

"But another man! You seed how Linn done!"

"I don' care. I love Willie-Ray."

"Willie Ray ain't no count. He don't care 'bout nothing but a jug a whisky or a crap game."

"Willie-Ray's good. He's good for me. I don' care what no body says, I'm gonna marry him." She was shouting now

And her mother shouted too. Tore her lungs,

Tubercular, at her daughter, at Clara:

"And what about Bill? You know Bill can't stan' him."

"Damn Bill. Damn all a' you. Ain't no body'll stop me."

"'At's the way you was with Linn, come dragging in, big as a barrel and you hardly grown. Now you cussing that boy to God Almighty. He can't help where he come from. And now you'll put Willie-Ray Perkins over him? I wouldn't treat a dog like that."

"I tol' you, Mama, I'm gonna marry Willie-Ray an' that all they is to it."

"Rule or ruin."

꙰

He grew up a city boy, that means, I guess,
he had a short childhood in the place
Where wildflowers bloom and grandmothers
Are kind as warm bathwater, then
Grew up sudden, with a jerk

Like reaching up too high when the football comes
And flesh tears itself, hanging in the air.

I see him in a schoolyard, roughing
With the rough boys the way
I never did, learning, I guess, his way
Of hitting, having racial hate
Put deeper down than reason ever could
Tear it out—Bill, my genes
Becoming not me, he who held
My mother, body into body, the way
I have never held a woman, and came
Flesh of her flesh—my flesh
My build, the way the Allen men
Run to fat in their forties.
From a drop we come, as Hillel said.

I saw a rainbow at midnight
Out on the deep blue sea...
They danced, my mother and father,
Before they were my mother and my father,
But two lost people, in love
And desire, in a honky tonk, in Jackson
To that song. She was to keep
The scratched '78 for years
And give it to me, to be mine,
And tell me it was their song
When lovers had songs
That silly lyric, crooned
In the style that was going
Out of style in 1946. She never

Said one bad thing about him, to me.

A rainbow at midnight, rainbow round the moon
I guessed it means. Dreams, it means,
Magic, how we wish this person
In our arms to be, not this person
But all our dreams come true. He held her
Wanting, wishing, the power of the wish
Bending existence till it is—
Clay in our hands becomes
Cups and jugs and pitchers. No,
She was not to be
Clay to his potter, human
She, from her soul,
He shaped nothing, from her clay,
Me, only me. Flesh
From a pouring, no. Bodies in bodies
Make bodies; babies, humans, poets
Are shaped with hands and words and food
Put to mouths and that hard love
Beyond the pleasant sway of the body
Dancing, dancing.

Ida was my mother, that blind old maid,
Jim my father and grandfather, Hazel's father; his hands
Held my hand to make letters, he sat
And fed me words, his was the thin
Switch on my legs when I needed
A switch on my legs, the aspirin when I was fevered,
The extra quilt when I was cold;
and Bevie too, who read me books,

Hour upon hour, before I could read—
These folks, my parents, the story
Of Bill and Hazel is the story of something else.

I have been cruel
To no one.
I have been cursed
                    To my face and my anger
                    Towered like a mushroom cloud
But I said nothing.
I am a Jones.

A rainbow at midnight? He had seen rainbows
      on the sea
On the troop ship, going to Japan
On a wide ocean, on a ship
With no women. Was there a man? That
Is in my genes too. Did he love
Some man a time, a while? Did his loins
That carried half of me, stir
Once maybe, in the shower?

Hazel waited back in the states
And a wife also. I think
He told her all, for she told me
Part, told her while their bodies moved
To music, and swore
He'd get a divorce when he could,
By mail, from occupied Japan.

And the letters came. I read a few

When I was hunting for who he was,
Or I was, but I could not
Bear to read the love talk
My parents made when I
Was only implicit in their desire.

Dearest Darling,

Will Drop you a few More lines from Okinawa and Darling I Must say its one torn up Place. From what I can see, theres several different Kind and Sizes of recked and torn up ships, and the land scape is sure ragid, and Ime not Kidding,

He wrote them long, had an eye for detail,
Couldn't spell, as I
Can't spell—On some island
Where there had been a fury
Of blood and fire while he
Was young and married with a child
In Chester County, he picked up
The skull of a Japanese soldier.
I see him hold it like Hamlet
His mirror in Yorrick—Where
Are the lips . . .

We had a show tonight out on the Sun deck But, it was too cold for me, I only saw a little of it, couldn't stand the Sea Breeze, Come back down in my quarters [?] & here I am wrighting you.

Just as I cannot stand the cold.

How wide the world must have been
To that boy from Chester County,
A great ruin to explore.

      Then there was a divorce, I suppose
           From that second wife,
        And coming home, I see him
For a while through Ida's eyes,
Blind, or Jim's jaundiced
To the man he did not want his daughter to marry.

He was always good to me, would lead me—
As I led her— I count Hazel was as much at fault
In that divorce.

One time him and Ed went hunting, down there towards
Beaver Creek, and durned if he didn't kill a fox and bring
it home to Hazel, asked her to cook it. Didn't know no
better 'an that!

so Darling you already Know how Deeply head over heels
Ime in Love With you, so you dont have that to Worry about,
So Be for Darling & My True Love
    Forever. Your G. I. "Bill"

—This to his third wife-to-be,
Third of five.

"Your honor," he said to the judge
In a paternity case for a daughter, "your honor
When you run through a briar patch
Do you notice which briar sticks deepest?"

Glenn, brief brother, a word for you.
I knew you for so few months
Before you died, and respected
You for how little you would tell
Of all the sorry truths you chose
To take to the grave. You
Were better than our father, or at least
Did him proud and made a life
In spite of all he did.

I braced you on your pillows
In the Jackson hospital
Where you were at a slow dying—
Flesh of my father
That never touched me—
I looked for recognition in your eyes, and think
I found it there, though we two
Had eaten one meal together in better days.
                    I put some ground ice to your lips.
And you died and I grieved
And felt whole for having known
Some living part of my father
That was not me.

One secret I have not told,
Here, in this poem,
Not because I am ashamed.
But for Glenn's sake.

I met a man from Jackson who said his name was Jack Barber, and he moved two fingers apart and together like scissors—"You know, like a barber—yeah, I knowed him. Red Allen, we called him, cause his hair was red. Him and me used to drive a taxi together, there in Jackson. There was a bar there on Royal Street and Red, he got a little too rowdy in there one time, so they throwed him out. Well, what did he do, but come back the next day with a shotgun and shoot the place all to pieces, shot through the walls, the counter and everything. Didn't hurt nobody, but he had to pay for all that."

Temper, blind temper
The ruin of him.
Like a bottomless void
      In him, the fury of his shaggy heart
        Moving, burning. It ruined
          His life, his life
And how many women
Did he hurt, leave
Like my mother?

While him and Hazel lived with us, we was raising a bunch a pig a old sow had. Bill was out there slopping 'em one day, and the old sow as she commenced to get up, stepped on one of her little ones. Well, Bill didn't have no more sense than to jump over there in with that old sow and she took out after him. He got back over the fence—a hog bite's a nasty thing to have, gets infected easy—'fore she could get to him, but then he grabbed a stick of stove wood and throwed it at that old sow. Broke her leg. We had to kill her, and her with them little pigs.

My cousin and my uncle and I
Put our heads together and count
Women, women he married, or might have married.
Poor chroniclers on the sidelines,
Counting, as though they were trophies—
How many? How many!

1605 North Grand

I went and found it with a city map,
The house where Bill, my dad, grew up.
He fled here, to his city aunt, this house
Whose bricks are wearing round, the moss
Creeps up them and the mortar's gone.

The house must have been old back when
He came from Chester County but then
He did not know the house, no more than I
Know this place where strangers live—
The house and land have passed from hand
To hand, each time legal, impersonal.

I guess he stood and stared out that window
And thought of a wooden house and a wide
Plank porch where Betty Lasiter his own
Grandmother sat and peeled off strips
Of 'tater skin and talked and sang.

He thought, I guess, about that day
They buried her, when he had walked
The graveyard lawn where I have walked
And read the tombstone names that I
Have read that meant to him his world
But are so little more than names to me.

A mind some half like mine moved on
The serried row of facts, but each
Small fact had then its own taste, smell

Peculiarity as that
Mind had. The book is lost, I know
No more than some bare list of contents,
The poetry is what he was.

I ask and ask and ask. But I
May ask these questions all day long.
I stare too long into a stranger's home.

↘

"Grrranpaw spent ta ta ta all his money hu-hu-hunting for
him." My cousin speaks, his voice so thick
I can hardly understand, but he, like me
Is the one who remembers, a gentle, single old man
Who knows the family story. I reflect
That it was the Depression that ruined
Hosea Attaway's business, not just hunting for
Grandpa Linn. I ask him how my father died,
Knowing only that it was an auto accident.
"He-he-he wuss in a '69 Chevelle
On the S-s-s-aint Louis Highway
Big truck got him. Ne-ne-ne-never did
Do no-no-nothing to the driver."
My old cousin reaches round
Touches my head on the left side, above the temple:
"Ca-ca-ca-ved in his head ri-ri-right there."

The Jackson Movie Theater

They used stone in those days, and stone
Outlives our uses. This theater
Is like some Roman ruin, where Caesars
Indulged their pride, and barbarians
Fed their mules and weeds
Grew through the Renaissance.
            Perhaps three
Businesses have been in this worn-out husk
Of stone since Humphrey Bogart
Smoked on the screen, and James Dean
Was doomed in celluloid.
                        Now
It's empty as a can the rats
Have licked out clean, and leaves
Like tired old women in drab coats
Cluster before the ticket counter
And rustle their gossip though the late summer wind.

I came and peered though the cracked glass door,
And saw, through my own dim reflection,
Only such junk inside as no one cared to steal.

I was looking for my father.

I guessed that he and Mother must
Have come to movies here,
Have waked this sidewalk
Before the roots of weeds cracked it up.

Across the street, the courthouse,
Where the divorce was, where the records of the divorce
Still are, I guess. I cannot stand to look
At them. I know what is in them.

His eye saw
The pink marble carvings before
The grime of forty years clung to them.
                    If I see
What he saw, hear the echoes
His shoes made between the cement
And corbelled tin ceiling,
Then I can guess for some small certainty
What he must have heard, seen through
Eyes much like mine, I guess, although
I never looked in them. In some almost way
I look out of them, and see
Beyond my transparent image
What Bill Allen never lived to see—
Ruins of the Jackson Movie Theater,
Without so much as one Olivier's ghost
To act out Hamlet for us now.

At the End

This is the end.
The voices that spoke
Speak no more.
        Silence is left
Full of the words spoken once.

They are all gone—
Bodies into dust
Souls into God
Words into silence.

The cracked voice that spoke
Has passed through these rhythms
Into an imminence of eternity.

Witness is the poet
They spoke through:

He says
Their aching gouts of pain
Have ceased all in a moment,
Have laid their hands
Into the hands of all the world.

They stand with long beards,
With pendulous dugs,
With callused hands, and wet diapers,
Humble gods,
        Convicting

All who walk the dust they walked,
All on whose faces the rain
Falls cold.
      Convicting
Of pride, and greed, if they look on life
For more than these simple chronicles.

Their gaze falls like sleet on all
Who want more than bread to eat,
And love, and a fire in the wintertime.

No bidding peace,
No farewell,
Forever are they with you
Dwelling in the hardness of life.

There comes all joy.
In that silence
All the stories are told
Unforgotten, forever.